THE BOUNDARY REVOLUTION

DECOLONIZE YOUR RELATIONSHIPS AND DISCOVER A NEW PATH TO JOY

JUDY HU, LMHC, BOUNDARY COACH

Difference Press

Washington, DC, USA

Published 2023

DISCLAIMER

Cover design: Jennifer Stimson

Editing: Natasa Smirnov

Author's photo courtesy of Wes Verge

*This book is dedicated to my children, Sofia and Kaia,
who broke open my heart so that I could become the mother
we all needed*

CONTENTS

AM I CRAZY?

Cathy reached out to me after a particularly dark moment with her children, who were five and three at the time. With deep shame, she admitted she had forcefully put her hands over her older son's mouth to get him to stop crying so he wouldn't wake his sister or annoy his father. It was the opposite of how she imagined behaving as a parent. She let go when she saw the horror in her son's eyes.

"The rage was so intense. I could see myself smothering him with a pillow. I can't believe I thought about doing that. I'm such a terrible mother!"

On the surface, she had a successful career at a renowned venture capital firm based in California. At the office, she was seen as smart, driven, confident, and decisive. Internally, she felt anxious and constantly overwhelmed, particularly at home. Between the incessant demands of her children and the relentless nature of her career, she was barely holding herself together. The dissonance between the perfect image she curated on social media and her internal experience often made her feel like a fraud.

The intensity of her stress paired with her husband's laid-back attitude made for very tense arguments. Cathy met her husband, David, at Harvard University, and both continued on to Harvard Business School. Like Cathy, David worked long hours, but he was not as emotionally available to co-parent as she needed.

I could hear her distraught voice as I read her email: "Something feels off. I love my kids, but they drive me crazy, and I constantly scream at them and feel so overwhelmed all the time. I need help managing my stress. Couples counseling hasn't helped my marriage. Can you help me?"

CONTEXT IS KEY

Like with all my clients, I started gathering Cathy's complete developmental history looking for how Cathy internalized her Self concept at her different childhood developmental stages. Then I gathered information about her family of origin three generations back to better understand her in the context of intergenerational familial patterns: for example, how her parents manage conflict and talk about feelings, and if there is any history of abuse, neglect, mental health issues, or addictions. Collaboratively, we placed her family within the context of what was happening in the social environment, such as whether there was war, immigration, poverty, and the like. Everything that might give further contour to her lived experience was taken into account.

Cathy was a forty-one-year-old first-generation Chinese-American cis-woman married to a forty-five-year-old Jewish American cis-man, David, from a prominent family in New Jersey. They had two children: Daniel (age five) and Joy (age three). Being happily married was Cathy's dream since childhood. Her parents were unhappily married, and she always felt like nothing she did was ever good enough to earn praise or acknowledgement. She learned at an early age to achieve and people please in order to keep things a bit calmer between her and her mother, who was highly critical of her appearance and demanded high achievement. Constantly expected to help with her little brother, Cathy couldn't wait to get out of her family to start her own life.

Cathy's first child, Daniel, was a handful. The bonding with him was difficult due to the emergency C-section, postpartum depression, and difficulty breastfeeding. When Joy was born two years later, Cathy was already medicated and seeing a therapist. The addition of Joy was a much easier experience compared to Daniel.

In the safety of our session, Cathy shared that she often dreaded time with Daniel, who likely sensed the difference in treatment and affection. She worried that Daniel would learn to walk on eggshells with her as Cathy tip-toed around her own mother. Cathy hated how reactive she was, but Daniel drove her crazy with his defiance and hyperactivity.

The partner dynamic is an important consideration, especially when understanding how power and privilege impact it. Cathy's husband, David, was the youngest of three boys in his family and worked in finance like his father. His mother was a stay-at-home parent who liked to throw lavish parties for her husband's colleagues. Being the youngest, he had a lot of freedom and took advantage of it until his mom had a mental breakdown. When Cathy suffered a late-term miscarriage before Daniel was born, David's mother disclosed that her breakdown was due to unprocessed grief from a stillbirth. Had the baby survived, she would have been David's older sister. Cathy shared that both she and David were worried about Cathy's mental health, but he didn't seem to change his behavior by spending more time with the family, which was what Cathy desperately needed.

Whenever Cathy tried to get David to understand how his lack of presence made it hard for her to parent in the way that she wanted, he got defensive and claimed that Cathy's standard of parenting and performing was too high. "You need to learn to relax and be much stricter on the children when they misbehave," he'd say matter-of-factly whenever Cathy sought empathy and validation. Neither of them had family close by, so the labor of child rearing and the household chores fell mostly on Cathy, like in many hetero-normative homes.

When David took responsibility for the children on the weekend so that Cathy could catch up on work, he claimed that Daniel was just fine. When describing her husband's approach, Cathy explained he was more relaxed, but clear with his expectations of the kids. "He gives them very few choices compared to me," she confessed.

As a hedge fund manager with remarkably long hours, he often prioritized resting on the weekend while Cathy wanted him to have quality time with the kids. Even though she was exhausted, she felt guilty if the kids didn't experience enriching outings with their dad, so she signed them up for activities, which David sometimes skipped without telling Cathy. More often than not, the family experienced big blowouts. At the start of the day, the blowouts were between Cathy and David, and at the end of the day between Cathy and her children. Forty-five minutes into our work together, she moved from sobbing and self-blaming to red-faced anger toward her husband for not believing in the invisible labor of women. Back and forth she went, looking for who was at fault. Hunched over her lap, cradling her face, she looked like a young child needing a soothing hug from a loving parent – something neither of her own parents ever offered.

Cathy was certain that she was the problem. Her indecisiveness, her disorganization, her anxiety, her uncontrollable outbursts directed at her children and husband were the obstacles she wanted to tackle in our work together. Her treatment goals were to be calmer and more focused so she could be a better mother and wife.

"I feel like I'm drowning and barely keeping my head above water. I'm ashamed that I sometimes hate my kids. I hate how my husband can be so relaxed when I'm basically doing a million things at once. I'm so tired all the time I want to cry. Why is it so hard for me? Am I crazy or just incompetent?"

I felt so much compassion for Cathy and predicted that her challenge with setting boundaries with her children and spouse likely extended into her work relationships as well.

Deciding to have children while working at her particular firm was nerve wracking. While other colleagues had been named Partner within five to six years, Cathy had yet to be promoted after seven years. When she became pregnant, she fielded questions from her boss like "Do you think you'll be as committed to your work?" Technically, these questions were borderline illegal, but unsurprising, since the audacity of the men at her firm was one of the stressors she identified.

At the close of one of our sessions, she admitted in a low whisper how deeply she regretted ever having children. She often dropped into deep shame whenever she caught herself fantasizing about her life prior to parenting. The feeling of being a failure both at home and at work often brought on suicidal ideations and panic. She equated failing to being worthless, which is understandable since that was exactly what her mother used to tell her if she came home with an A minus.

"What happened to me? I question every decision I make now. One of my children needing to stay home from daycare when they get sick will push me over the edge. I was never like this before. What is wrong with me? My husband looks at me like I'm crazy and I'm starting to believe he may be right."

YOU ARE NOT CRAZY

Listening to Cathy talk about her childhood brought me back to why I changed the way I work as a mental health clinician. Her story is so similar to so many of my other clients: high achievers with difficulty setting boundaries, conflict-avoidant, stressed, and lonely. Cathy isn't crazy. The world in which Cathy lives is crazy.

Let me explain.

Remember how context is key? Our context in the United States is a result and perpetuation of colonization by way of white body supremacy. Let me get us on the same page: Colonization is the desire to establish permanent settlements in a foreign land and eventually control the land and its people, the indigenous people. Furthermore, those sent to colonize for the British Empire were themselves subjected to violence and profound neglect back home. In trying to emulate the elite class by way of owning land and enslaving people, they centered the very trauma they endured back in Europe by deeming others disposable. As a result of being dehumanized themselves, objectifying another human seemed not only normal, but also necessary. Everyone in this oppressive system has been harmed. Not only have we as a society learned to tolerate violence, neglect, and exploitation, but we have learned that it is status quo.

The history of the United States is the history of colonization on one land, over different groups of people, over and over again. When I talk about decolonizing relationships, this is what I mean: in the same way that colonization controlled land and people, so too does this worldview control how we think about our Selves, or who and how we perceive ourselves at our core. If you subjugate yourself to emulate the elite class, the Colonizer covertly retains their control and power over you because they will maintain and perpetually manipulate the standard by which you will be assessed and deemed worthy. This way of thinking demands constant appraisal of your Self-worth, which then impacts how you relate to others, because in order to regain a sense of control, people will often resort to oppressing others since that now seems like the "normal" way to live.

My teacher, author and fellow trauma therapist Resmaa Menakem, brilliantly explains: "Trauma decontextualized in a person looks like personality. Trauma decontextualized in a family looks like family traits. Trauma decontextualized in a group of people looks like culture." This has been my compass as I've been decolonizing my body and mind from the generational impact of trauma and oppression.

When we experience a physical trauma, our body centers that experience in order to heal it. For instance, if I sprain my ankle, my body changes the way it moves to compensate for the sprain in order to allow it to heal, thus centering the wound. Emotional trauma, as I'm describing it now, is something that is too much, too soon, and too fast for the body, mind, and spirit to integrate in a healthy way; it feels like you are all alone in surviving the experience. As it does with the sprained ankle, the body centers the emotional trauma as well in an attempt to heal. Without context, the body can personalize the emotional trauma in order to gain a sense of control. Consider, as an example, a child who lost a grandparent during the pandemic. Decontextualized, this trauma could be internalized in a way that makes the child believe that connecting to others in any way is unsafe and likely lead to getting sick. As a result, the child's behavior may present as social anxiety unless and until a caring adult can coach the child through the experience.

Our bodies and brains are wired to survive. Like other animals, we are incredibly resilient. We can adapt to accommodate the impact of trauma, and our bodies can then pass down that adaptation to our children epigenetically without our realizing. In this way, the legacy of trauma can be passed down generation after generation.

In research done on lab mice, mice were trained

to fear the smell of cherry blossoms because when the scent of cherry blossoms was released into the cages, the mice would receive an electric shock. After ten days, only the scent was released with no electric shock, yet the mice would continue to retreat to the sides of the cage in fear. Those mice were then bred. When the next generation of mice smelled cherry blossoms, they instinctively responded in fear even though they never experienced the electrical shock. This is epigenetics in a nutshell: behaviors and environment can cause changes that impact how your genes work, and thus how you - and your descendants - behave or perceive your environment.

We see this same passing on of trauma in the families of those who survived the Holocaust. The grandchildren of survivors presented symptoms of post-traumatic stress disorder (PTSD). Without the larger context, these grandchildren's struggles could seem like a mental health issue, but in reality, it is their bodies' way of trying to center the trauma in order to heal it.

Trained as a mental health counselor, I - and others in my field with similar professional foundations - have been misunderstanding the cues. The focus has been on the symptoms rather than the root cause. My concern now is that the goal of mental health counseling too often has been to get clients well enough to go back to work by managing symptoms rather than healing the root cause.

Let's look at a recent collective trauma, like COVID-19. Over 1 million people have died in the US alone. The death toll is over 6 million worldwide. Currently, there is a spike in children and adults being diagnosed with anxiety, depression, and ADHD. The wait times for therapy and residential treatment facilities are appalling. When we look at these symptoms out of context, it can look like personality – "these people are suffering from anxiety disorders and depression" –rather than understanding that these are reasonable responses to a traumatic event like the isolation of lockdown, food/housing insecurity, sudden death of a loved one, or witnessing the murders of countless Black and brown men, women, and children. Having such a narrow focus on symptoms and adaptations will miss the mark on getting to the root cause, hindering true healing.

Not so long ago, I myself missed the mark in my own life. As I was struggling with intense reactivity and constant suicidal ideation, I feared that I would harm my children. I interpreted every struggle in them as a failure in me. My focus was to find what was wrong with me and fix it. On the other side of that crisis, I now understand that my suicidal ideation was my body's way to seek relief from my constant self-criticism and doubt. Looking back, I feel so grateful that I was able to shift the focus from blaming my Self as the issue and instead consider the environment in which I was trying to live my life. Thankfully, I discovered that the way I was living my life, assessing my life, was killing me. My pain has given me a road map, and now I am committed to offering others this new path towards joy and authenticity.

My hope is that this book will show you the steps to revolutionize the way you approach boundaries by deconstructing and decolonizing the ways you were taught to relate to your Self and each other.

Remember: You are not crazy. You are not defective. You are not alone. I am here to tell you that I am with you on this path. I myself am deeply flawed and hope that you feel comforted knowing that I have been where Cathy is, and I know how to navigate us through it.

2

AM I ENOUGH?

y suicidal ideations often came to me as a fantasy of stepping in front of a bus, or dying from a heart attack, or getting a terminal cancer diagnosis. These fantasies brought me brief moments of relief that were then immediately followed by intense shame. These were hopeless moments that I used to think indicated something was wrong with me. *Is it my depression coming back? Why is everything so hard for me? Why am I so broken?*

The self-criticism Cathy used to describe herself sounded so similar to my inner assessment of my character: *Crazy, fraud, worthless, defective, weak, messy, disorganized, stupid, incompetent.* If I, Cathy, and count-less other clients use that exact same language, then there's a larger question to ask: Why? Why do so many people, particularly those of color, feel this way in their lives?

For me, I learned to tolerate disappointing myself at every point in my life because I could not tolerate anyone's disappointment in me, especially my mother's since she would often threaten to self-harm or disown me if I did not meet her expectations. As a result, someone's anger at setting a boundary, or my children's whining about my "no," were simply intolerable in my body – it felt as if someone's life was at risk.

Instead, I prioritized centering someone else's comfort over my own. That behavioral pattern I learned in my family fit nicely in the American cultural expectation that women, particularly mothers, should sacrifice everything for their children and husbands. It should be no surprise that as I slowly steered away from my Self, I ended up creating a life I hated living.

What I know now is that those suicidal ideations and fantasies were my body's way to tell me: *The life you built is killing you.*

Cathy's rock-bottom moment was firmly silencing her son with her harsh hand. Mine was when I raged at my children at the dinner table, shattered a dish in the sink, and then ran upstairs to calm down. The image of tiny little fingers pushing a piece of paper underneath the locked bathroom door is still so clear: "Dear Mom, do you like me?"

I can still remember the quiet gasp and holding of my breath while seeing my daughter's note, followed by sobbing and the all-too-familiar sense of shame. There was a place in my heart where I knew I loved my children, but every inch of my body loathed parenting them. My brain couldn't reconcile having these two opposing experiences simultaneously all the time.

What I realize now is that I dreaded any sort of relationship where I needed to ask for help, set a boundary, tolerate someone else's disappointment, or be vulnerable.

In my brain, there was a picture of what parenting was supposed to look like, but parenting actual children was excruciating for me. Like Cathy's challenging relationship with Daniel, I parented a child who triggered my own trauma history. She was explosive, inattentive, defiant, and incredibly attuned to my moods. At that time, I was a therapist who helped people with parenting challenges. I felt like such a fraud!

As a child, I would have written a slightly different note to my mother: "Mom, why don't you love me? What can I do to make you love me?"

Before we go any further in this chapter, I want to be clear that this story is not intended to berate anyone, including myself, and especially not my mother. I share my experience openly because I want to destigmatize the struggle of mental health while also contextualizing the behavioral and cultural adaptations that result from intergenerational trauma. There is no "bad guy" in this book – only humans behaving imperfectly, often feeling lost, alone and desperate … humans needing hope, healing, connection, and a different path forward.

MY CONTEXT

My family's origin story began in China, well before I even existed as a possibility. After World War II, Communism took control over China. My father was traveling overseas with his father and an older sister when the borders closed. My dad was the youngest of his siblings—the only boy—and was never able to say goodbye to his mother or other siblings.

Later, my mother would travel with her mother and brother to visit their father on "holiday" without realizing that they were actually fleeing China in order to reunite with her dad who was also locked out of China. After many years apart, the family resettled in Taiwan. Six months after my mom's sister was born, my grandfather would die suddenly in an accidental fall, leaving behind a widow with partially bound feet, and now, three children in a foreign land with very little access to money, resources, and support.

Poverty, war, and the impact of the Cultural Revolution left lasting traces in my epigenetics. My mother's tiger parenting was a direct result of her missed opportunity for an education, and the very real opportunities for an education overseas given only to those who earned the highest marks. Perfection was not only a goal; it was literally a ticket to survival.

Due to many different factors, including patriarchy and poverty, my mother was forced to marry the man who raised me. My dad was eighteen years her senior. As an adult now, I can see that her frustration and disapproval *of* me had little to do *with* me and much more to do with her own unprocessed trauma and lost opportunities to create a life of her choosing.

Children, with their limited brain development, create belief systems about how the world works. My childhood belief was centered around being unwanted and a burden to others. In times of stress, my mother would lash out to relieve some pressure: "This is all your fault! I am so miserable. If you weren't here I could leave. I wish you were never born!" As an adult, I now understand that her words were a trauma reaction. While she didn't really mean what she said, the impact on my development was real and long lasting.

Being raised in my family's Chinese restaurant, I learned how to be invisible and helpful to my family. I earned high praise for having no needs or demands. Flexibility, silence, and perseverance were badges of honor. As a first grader, I remember feeling pride when I declined playdate invitations because I needed to work. In middle and high school, I applied that behavior of playing small and agreeable to my peer relationships. As an adult, being a hard-working agreeable woman with no demands also afforded me high praise at work. It makes sense that I would naturally decenter, or render myself invisible, within my newly developing nuclear family. I believe Cathy was doing the same in her own family, as many women do unconsciously due to cultural and patriarchal messaging from countless generations. Martyrdom, sacrifice, and selflessness earn the highest of praise.

Parents and children are wired to bond with each other. Children require a parent to provide them with care in order to survive. As a child, I longed to be loved. I imagined finding a husband, having beautiful children, and living the Martha Stewart lifestyle I witnessed in advertisements and movies. As an adult, whenever I wouldn't achieve the "look" of that fantasy, I felt like something was wrong with me. *Why can't I achieve that feeling? Why is it so hard to plan the day? What is wrong with me?*

This drive to compare myself with others was ingrained in me. My parents often compared me and my sibling as a way to motivate each of us to do better. That comparison left very little space to have a sibling relationship with each other. Instead, it motivated us to compare, belittle, and compete with each other to fight over the little affection and approval that was available.

This relationship dynamic with my brother is one of my first experiences of two conflicting desires: pleasing my parents made me feel good and loved, but ensured passive-aggressive interactions with my brother, who subsequently felt alienated and unloved. Disappointing my parents would feel life-threatening, but would provide some relief from the snide comments I received under my brother's breath.

Being the first in my family to be born in America, I embodied the hyphen in Chinese-American. My nervous system wired itself around the function of holding two differing identities effortlessly, all while not belonging anywhere. Be invisible and helpful.

Rather than talk with me about my cultural identity, my dad would often tease me, "Are you Chinese-American or American-Chinese?" Viscerally, the answer was neither. I just felt this emptiness internally that I longed to fill.

Not Chinese enough and not American enough. That familiar feeling of *not enoughness*, that longing to belong – to be wanted – somewhere, was mapped in my body.

It's no surprise that I pursued the elusive goal of contentment. Once I get a good job, I will feel good enough. Once I get married, I will feel good enough. Once I have kids, I will feel good enough. Once I have a clean and organized house with joyous family meals, I will feel good enough.

As a chronic people pleaser, parenting triggered my trauma history constantly. I perceived my typical children as distracted and non-compliant children whose choices in behavior reflected directly on my success or failure as a parent. My husband worked very long hours, so I was often alone with my parenting struggles. When I talked to my fellow mom friends, they would commiserate but not seem as nearly distraught or miserable as I was.

Waking to the thought *I hate my life* is a little disconcerting as a mental health clinician, but I ignored it since that thought was a familiar one since childhood. I learned to acknowledge the thought and just override it. Resilience also earns high praise.

Looking back on my life as an adult, where I am now, I understand that my mother parented from a place of what she thought she was supposed to be – how to look successful, how to look confident. Having successful children based on some fantasy created a sense of success in her. So, it is not surprising that I adopted a similar standard of success: *Don't disappoint anyone.* I oriented my success, my goodness, my *enoughness*, around pleasing every single person around me, except me.

THE PSYCHOLOGICAL BOUNDARIES FRAMEWORK™

Thankfully, I'm not new to therapy. It is vital for a therapist to regularly do one's own emotional healing work so that we don't inadvertently retraumatize our clients. During my rock bottom, I attended a workshop called "Healing Our Core Issues," led by a local therapist and author Jan Bergstrom. The way Jan presented Inner Child work clicked for me and allowed me to integrate different pieces of my own clinical training and personal healing to create my Psychological Boundaries Framework™. My approach incorporates the nuanced impact of power, privilege, and oppression (e.g., race, class, sexual orientation, gender identity, body ability, mental health, et cetera) on relational dynamics that undoubtedly impact how you view yourself, your value, and your needs.

As a Licensed Mental Health Counselor, I was used to working long term (three-plus years) with clients, either weekly or biweekly. As a trauma survivor who needs to actively manage my chronic depression and anxiety, I used to believe I would need therapy for the rest of my life, a belief that others might share. Before I developed this new way of seeing my Self, I was easily triggered and reactive, and many a time counted down the days until I could see my therapist.

Even though some of my therapists unintentionally gaslit my experience because they didn't understand the impact of race and privilege, I couldn't imagine not having the support of therapy. I wasn't used to having any support, so paying someone to support me felt easier. Additionally, I never questioned or challenged any of my therapists. I basically needed a replacement mother figure who could offer love that I didn't experience with my actual mother. Some of my client relationships felt a similar way – many of them looking to me, their therapist, for assurance that they were good enough, loveable, and making the "right" decision.

It's interesting to me how long I believed that that type of codependence or reliance on a therapist seemed appropriate. My training was to diagnose and treat the "disorder." But once I developed, practiced, and honed my *Psychological Boundary Framework*, which involved seeing people locked in a context that was put on them in childhood as opposed to via the lens of a disorder, I noticed a shift in my body in relation to my clinical work.

With this style of deconstruction, I started feeling

more energized and less burned out. Before, the level of stress I put on myself to "heal" my clients was unsustainable, grandiose, and unhealthy. I would feel like a good therapist if my client felt good. I would feel like a bad therapist if my client felt bad. This level of enmeshment and codependence, where my sense of esteem relied on outside factors, was incredibly familiar and absolutely toxic.

What often took years of treatment now only needs around six months to a year of boundary healing, practice, and integration. Seeing my clients change their lives from the inside out, as I did, is rewarding but no longer the basis of my self-esteem. My clients learn that fact, too: they are the ones that they have been waiting for, not their parent, not their partner, not their child, not their work, not their bank account, and certainly not their therapist.

I now understand and respect every person I come into contact with by seeing their humanity and trusting that they are doing the best that they can with what they have. I no longer elevate myself over them by judging their choices. I no longer shrink down my worth if someone judges me. Of course, there is no end point in our healing journey, but applying this framework has increased my sense of agency, my authenticity, and my joy.

Healing my boundaries allowed a profound shift in my body in relation to my own trauma. Historically, I centered my trauma and focused my life on healing myself. Now, after practicing what I preach, I center my Self and focus on living my life. Healing is not my life's purpose; living my life is. Sure, I still get triggered and have really bad days, but I know how to get through it now without needing to fantasize about my death.

The life I live now is far from picture perfect because perfection is not the goal. For me and my clients, the goal is living in one's full authenticity, which includes the spectrum of experiences and emotions, including the messy and hard ones. Yes, I still have moments of overwhelm and losing my temper. The current state of the world is both overwhelming and infuriating, and I am teaching my children how to see the world as it is – broken and beautiful. I am teaching them it is our responsibility to collectively heal it by starting internally.

Not only are my relationships healthier and no longer codependent, but the joy I feel is boundless. The boundaries I set and the conversations I have are much more honest and connected. For the first time in my life, I feel like I know myself, have my own back, and can hold myself and others accountable without shaming myself or blaming others. Experiencing my internal liberation, witnessing the awakening of my clients, and accompanying my children on their journey, rather than controlling it, has made me so hopeful for our future.

My goal with Boundary Coaching is to foster the healing of psychological boundaries–to get everyone back to their "right size," which is valued equal to another regardless of class, race, gender, sexual orientation, et cetera. It is helpful to see what this looks like in practice. When someone has been used to having power and privilege, shrinking the space they can take up will feel oppressive and uncomfortable. That is okay. You may have been elevated and prioritized too much. In contrast, when someone is used to having very little power or privilege, expanding the space they can take up might feel aggressive and uncomfortable. That is also okay. If you were taught to devalue yourself, you need to learn to embody your full humanity without repeating the collective trauma of being oppressed or oppressing others. For example, when I work with couples where one partner is white and the other is a person of color, I compassionately call out entitlement and privilege while highlighting how the marginalized partner might unconsciously gaslight or minimize their own needs, enabling the cycle of oppression to continue.

Integral to the *Psychological Boundaries Framework* approach is the context in which we currently live, so I coach my clients when to use their privilege strategically. With one interracial lesbian family, I instructed the white wife to go and advocate for their biracial child at school for being bullied, rather than her non-binary Black partner. If dismissed or challenged, this white partner is much more emotionally resourced and will not be as triggered as her Black partner, whose response would likely be perceived as too aggressive. Many people of color understand that the white partner will always be taken more seriously.

When life gets messy and infuriating, I remind myself and my clients to go through the steps I am about to teach you in this book; and more often than not, I can get back on track. My goal with this book is to help you embody a new worldview that is grounded in equality, non-violence, freedom, social responsibility, and interdependence by uncovering the ways you've needed to adapt in order to survive within the larger context of your family and society. Decolonizing your sense of Self re-centers your humanity, in turn centering the humanity of others.

3

HOW OPPRESSION STUNTS CHILDHOOD DEVELOPMENT

In an ideal world, children's needs are prioritized because children are completely vulnerable and dependent on their adult caregivers. Centering children would mean that society provides adults with ample social support – ensuring that those adults are resourced enough to then provide the physical, psychological, and emotional needs for the youth. Meeting the basic needs of housing security, nutrient-dense food, safety from intentional harm, access to affordable universal healthcare, and good education would allow caregivers the emotional capacity to provide the patience and guidance that all children *require*. With resourced adults, kids can then safely explore, make mistakes, receive guidance, properly repair, and gradually mature into adulthood.

Unfortunately, we do not live in an ideal world. Instead of the most vulnerable, we center the wants of the wealthiest to help them gain more power and resources. With a slight of hand, we have been tricked to pursue a toxic fantasy of success and false empowerment by oppressing others. Due to the rat race of consumerism and capitalism, society needs children to be seen but not heard.

Human brains don't fully develop until their mid-twenties. While some animals like colts and lambs can begin walking shortly after birth, humans cannot. Human babies are born requiring caretaking and guidance for at least twenty years. Developmentally, children are tasked with the discovery of who they are, learning how to be in the world without harming others or allowing harm. Then, they must determine how to contribute to our world in a meaningful way that centers the needs of our future generations. Our society does not make this work easy. In fact, the societal expectations placed on our children to sit still and learn a certain way are not only unreasonable, but harmful: they prevent children from taking the proper developmental steps toward growing into mature adults. Since most adults, let alone children, do not understand that these expectations are inappropriate and harmful, children, like many adults, often internalize that there is something wrong with them, which is not the case.

It is the society that is wrong.

When every child understands that they are born inherently worthy – no more and no less worthy than any other human on this planet – we will be closer to a more peaceful and equitable society. You are enough as you are, regardless of race, socioeconomic status, religion, immigration status, sexual or gender identity, physical or mental ability, size, achievement, failure, et cetera. That inherent worth not only applies to every other human being on this planet, but it also applies to the other living creatures, and the Earth itself. We are but a part of a living ecosystem—a piece of a larger, intricate and perfect whole.

This chapter explains the developmental tasks that get bypassed when we fail to center the most vulnerable. By centering the wants of the wealthiest, we model how to oppress and fight for resources rather than guide our children towards the emotional and psychological maturity needed to create sustainable communities.

In looking at the ways that my clients and I adapted to endure childhood within these oppressive systems, I can understand the context in which these adaptations are now the obstacles preventing us from our full expression and undermining our potential for relational healing and true intimacy.

My framework labels the adaptations in each

developmental stage as Inner Children: "Wounded Baby," "Adaptive Child," "Adaptive Tween," and "Adaptive Teen." Then, in Chapters 4 to 8, I discuss the needed response to heal and reparent these inner children in order to mature into a functional adult. I use the term "Functional Adult" to mean someone who is committed to equality, non-violence, freedom, social responsibility, and interdependence.

Inner child work is a powerful way to reparent ourselves in order to heal the wounds we received in childhood due to the trauma endured from society. This inner healing essentially stops the legacy of collective trauma we pass on to our children. When we begin to heal those Inner Children, we heal our psychological boundary, change how we view our sense of Self, show up more authentically in the world, and relate to others with healthy boundaries. In healing our Selves, we heal the world.

BABY (CONCEPTION - PRESCHOOL) – MY WORTH IN THIS WORLD

The task of this developmental stage is to begin to conceptualize our sense of Self based on how our caregiver responds to us—as if a mirror reflecting our worth and lovability.

Current research shows that even in utero, babies are directly impacted by the emotional, psychological, and physical state of the pregnant parent. So, if the soon-to-be parent is excited and supported about the upcoming newborn, the brain will release hormones that support that excitement and anticipated joy. This essentially communicates to the growing fetus: *You are welcome and wanted. You are loved.*

In this stage of development from conception to before the child goes to school, the child is basically a sponge. Babies and toddlers have no emotional or psychological boundary because it is impossible for them to protect themselves at all. They are completely vulnerable and dependent on their care-givers and immediate environment. Based on the facial expression of the caregiver, tonal response, and physical connection, the child will personalize and internalize the caregiver's responses as truths about them. This is the start of the foundation of a child's sense of Self and the world.

The brain development in young childhood is so limited that children often have magical thinking, where a child believes that they are the center of the universe and personalizes everything, confident that they know the truth about the world. These worldviews can often look like: *The world is safe. I am good.* If the baby is planned and has received prenatal care and consistent food, shelter, protec-tion, and soothing, the child will likely experience and perceive their own inherent worth in the world, and trust that the world and people in it are safe and loving.

Let's take a look at the other extreme, like when the pregnancy is unplanned, unwanted, undernourished, or developing during a stressful time like in the cases of rape, domestic violence, poverty, famine, a pandemic, war, or while seeking asylum. The stress hormones of cortisol and adrenaline will have a direct impact on the developing fetus. The message the fetus might receive is: *I am unwanted. I am unsafe. I am a problem.*

If after the baby is born and the caregivers are unable to provide consistent food, shelter, or are abusive and/or neglectful, with unhealthy boundaries, then the young child will likely believe that the world and the people in it are unsafe because their needs are not important enough to be met. Their worldview might be: *The world is not safe. I am only worthy of love if I behave / look a certain way. My needs are not important. I do not matter.*

As an example, my mom's pregnancy with me was during an incredibly stressful time. Only as an adult looking back can I now understand that her desperation was not because of me personally, even though she often said it was. Following her husband, she was forced to leave Taiwan, her second home after fleeing Communism in China, in order to immigrate to a third country, America. Here, her husband forbade her to learn English or have control of the finances because he was almost two decades older than my mother, who was only nineteen when they married. He likely worried that if my mother had enough education and economic means, she might leave him. It was in that stressful situation that I was conceived, born, and raised, which contextualizes my deep-seated belief that I was unwanted.

So, what happens when the tasks of a particular developmental stage get bypassed? Well, we adapt, of course. Adaptations are necessary when the ideal environment is not possible. The problem is that these adaptations impact our maturation process by keeping us emotionally and psychologically stunted at different developmental stages.

Let's start from the earliest stage.

The Wounded Baby

Adapted from a model for healing childhood trauma work I learned from my workshop with Jan Bergstrom, I refer to the "Wounded Baby" as the adaptation or negative belief from the very start of your life. This idea of a Wounded Baby can be particularly powerful for people who have been adopted and have little to no information about the circumstances of their relinquishment by their birth parent.

For me, my baby Self adapted by becoming essentially invisible to make up for the fact that I was unwanted. As I was completely vulnerable to the moods of those around me and suffered from verbal and physical harm as well as emotional neglect, I learned to be needless and wantless, and only to do what was asked of me. Asking for help or initiating an idea often put me in the line of someone's fire. I was not free to explore or identify anything that brought me joy because that level of freedom did not exist in my family. We were barely getting by financially, and we lived in a predominantly white community. Of course, my Wounded Baby always felt like an inconvenience, a burden. My parents were not resourced enough. In order to justify my existence on this planet, I adapted by developing my ability to be helpful to those around me because my parents needed the support.

If I did everything my mother wanted, perhaps then she would be happy. But the poverty that forced her into marriage had lasting effects that were not considered in my magical thinking due to limited brain development at that age. I believed, and was often told, that my mere existence was burdensome. When someone has not done the work of inner decolonization, it makes sense that they would see oppressing another person as a way to enable a sense of power and control.

Hurt people hurt people.

In the process of my boundary healing, I realize now that it was not me and my inadequacy that victimized her. It was long standing patriarchy and the impact of Japan's brutal occupation of China between 1931 and 1945, where China claims 35 million Chinese were killed or wounded during the Japanese occupation, and subsequent political and social upheaval when the Chinese Communist Party gained control after defeating Japan. My mother was born in 1948. While she couldn't know the larger context that surrounded her, she absorbed the belief that male children were more revered in China because property followed the male line and females were married and joined to their husband's family. As a female child, my mother lacked any agency in her life. I was an easier and more immediate target than the unprocessed trauma of Japan's colonization of China, and the generational system that left so many women dependent on men and the prospects afforded from a marriage.

During my "Healing Our Core Issues" workshop, Jan Bergstrom guided me through a visualization where I imagined the hospital in which I was born. I imagined walking into the elevator and walking down the corridor to the room where my mom was recovering from her labor and delivery. Entering that room as an adult, I explained to my mother that I was there to claim my Self as a baby. Intuitively, I acknowledged that my mother didn't really want to have children since she never had her own childhood and did not fully consent to her arranged marriage with my father. I then reached down and picked up a swaddled baby and stared into her eyes, my beautiful baby eyes. Holding myself as a newborn, I showered her with the love and welcome she never received. Leaving the room and then the hospital, I could feel my mother's relief and my own at finally being claimed, loved, and free.

While emotionally exhausted from sobbing, I felt something unshackle within myself. It was the first time I could see myself as wanted and cherished because I wanted her, my Wounded Baby. I could reprogram my infant experience by receiving her cries with gentleness and care. After that workshop, I noticed that I no longer enter spaces and try to sense if my presence is welcome. From that moment on, while aware of my safety as an Asian-American woman, I now walk knowing I am fully entitled to exist and take up space. No longer needing to justify my existence in the world, I began living and loving my life.

YOUNG CHILD (PRESCHOOL - ELEMENTARY): MY PLACE IN THE WORLD

The task of our brains in young childhood is to form beliefs about the environment and our sense of Self in it. We take in immediate data we receive and create beliefs about our Self from our immediate family and the environment when we leave our home.

Ideally, children are allowed to develop physically and emotionally within a safe and containing environment at their own pace and in their own way. Through interactions with the caregivers and our environment, children should learn that they are precious, allowed to make mistakes, are protected from abuse and neglect, invited to explore what brings them joy, and that they exist with others who are equally as precious as they are and have the same protections and rights.

These early messages the child receives from their family of origin and society are internalized as world-views; beliefs about how the world works are akin to computer programming. The brain's programming computes: *Am I safe? Am I loved? Can I get my needs met? Am I allowed to be the center of the universe? Am I allowed to make mistakes? Can I ask for help? Can I be free to be me?* Those answers become the worldview – the computer program – in that child's brain. The brain then filters and processes the data that validates that particular belief system and *only* that data.

If the brain's computer program that started in your toddler years at home was that you were cherished and protected, then you expect to be cherished and respected in your peer relationships and with teachers at school. Those will be the people to whom you are drawn because those types of relationships and behaviors support your belief system. In contrast, if you learned to believe that you are a burden, then based on neutral data around you, you would only focus on the relationships that reinforce that you are a burden. For me, rather than connect with the friends who happily reached out to play with me, my brain fixated on the one person who not only refused to play with me, but also rolled their eyes whenever I asked to play. Annoyance was often how I was received by my mother and brother, so that peer's eye roll, while hurtful, felt familiar and thus, comfortable.

The Adaptive Child

The term "Adaptive Child" describes the ways you needed to adapt in order to survive as a young child.

Due to the circumstances in my family, particularly with my mother's unhealed trauma and how it manifested in her parenting of me, I believed that I was unwanted, burdensome, and ugly. I needed to be perfect to avoid rejection. I was not allowed to protect myself or have any boundaries because I was expected to be needless and wantless. Expressing my authenticity, including my vulnerabilities, would ensure that I not only would be rejected, but I would jeopardize the emotional stability of my caregiver, which felt life-threatening.

For example, my mother was a top student in her elementary school and demonstrated huge potential. When her father died suddenly in an accident, she needed to leave school so she could take care of her infant sister while their mother went out to work. My mom took great pride in sacrificing for the family and swallowed her bitter resentment that she could not continue in school. In early elementary school, while learning cursive and trying so hard to have perfect penmanship, I pressed down too heavily with my pencil so the lead smeared across the page, and the teacher reprimanded my handwriting and marked it unsatisfactory. My mother punished me harshly, leading me to believe I could never receive an unsatisfactory grade again because she threatened either self-harm or to disown me if I ever wasted my opportunity again. I believe now that my mother took out her unprocessed grief on me. Because she was not allowed to protect herself as a child and instead was praised to be needless and wantless, she expected her daughter to behave the same way. But as a child, not knowing her context, her behavior left a strong impression on me. My Adaptive Child learned to be achievement oriented, to ignore my own needs, and to be hypervigilant against disappointing anyone.

TWEEN (MIDDLE – HIGH SCHOOL): WHO I AM IN THE WORLD

This developmental stage between childhood and young adulthood is called the "tween" years, when puberty matures the body so it can reproduce. It is also the time for tweens to explore their identity and figure out who they are by surrounding themselves with lots of differing beliefs and expressions so they can develop their sense of Self within the bounds of social interactions and feedback. Exploring values and beliefs that are different from their family of origin is important and appropriate. The task of tweens is to physically and emotionally mature and explore who they are and how they would like to express their sense of Self in their life.

This stage of development is when the child's focus shifts from relying on their primary caregivers for support and security to peer groups as a means of survival. Whereas young children are wired to bond with their caregivers as a survival instinct because to be abandoned as a young child would mean imminent death, tweens need their friends. Since we are social creatures, finding a sense of belonging in a pack or group increases our chances of survival. Being isolated or socially rejected at this age feels like an existential crisis because it would have been for pack animals--the isolated or rejected individuals made the easiest target to prey upon.

Again, human brains do not fully develop until about mid-twenties. Yes, puberty enables our tween bodies to reproduce, but there is at least another decade needed for the maturation of the brain. To expect a tween to behave like an adult is not only unreasonable, it is extremely harmful.

Our society pushes our children to mature faster than they are emotionally capable of doing. This messy, awkward middle, if bypassed or rushed, means that our child likely builds an identity that is based on being accepted rather than on an authentic expression of their Self. Even though the tweens focus on social groups, tweens, like teens, still need the safety and guidance from their caregiver to discern the data they are collecting in a way that honors who they are meant to be. The focus needs to be on accepting themselves, so that they find resonance in their social group. Staying aligned to who they are will naturally attract affirming peers.

The Adaptive Tween

If the caregiver is not emotionally mature and safe, then oftentimes children learn to mask and behave inauthentically to avoid the disappointment, rejection, harm, or anger of their caregiver. If the child has had to mask in order to stay "safe" with their caregivers, then they will likely continue masking in their tween years in an attempt to be accepted into a social group. Since belonging is so vital to a healthy sense of Self, the Adaptive Tween likely prioritizes approval over authenticity in order to belong. Interpersonal conflicts increase because their boundaries hit up against another person's, and here begins the practice of negotiation in peer relationships. This conflict, while difficult and uncomfortable, is necessary and important to build interpersonal skills and learn effective communication. Adaptive Tweens might acquiesce and pretend to agree with the group in order to prevent conflict, or apply peer pressure by ostracizing and shaming another peer to distract from their own insecurity, thus repeating the harm inflicted by a condescending caregiver.

Born and raised in a predominantly white community validated the belief that I was ugly and unwanted. Because I grew up working class and working in our family restaurant, I was very socially awkward, only knowing how to serve rather than to self-advocate. I looked up to others as much smarter and better than me because my peers had a lot more freedom, resources, and social capital. Based on my experience as a child, I tolerated people treating me poorly if it meant I could be part of the group. I often bought lavish gifts for my friends because I needed to justify why they would want to spend time with me. I remember going to friends' houses and being in utter disbelief about how their home was so calm and supportive. My immature brain internalized that it was due to their supremacy that I needed to emulate. So, I became a chameleon and morphed into whomever I was around at any given point in time. If I was with friends who were interested in romantic partners, my Adaptive Tween would twirl my hair and talk about boys too, even though I wasn't interested. If other friends weren't interested in grades, my Adaptive Tween pretended to not care while secretly staying up all night to complete assignments.

TEENS (POST HIGH SCHOOL - MID 20S): HOW AND WHY I AM IN THE WORLD

This stage of development is when teenagers through young adulthood are supposed to differentiate fully from their parents so that they may express who they are by creating their own life that excites them and gives them a sense of purpose in the world. Most often, teenagers internalize and integrate the ways they were parented and treated in school while learning how to see, respect, and negotiate with their peers. They practice being adults while still having access to the emotional support and coaching from caregivers.

The Adaptive Teen

For parents who stay enmeshed, these teens are often anxious and fearful of trying new things, especially if it means they might fail. For parents who are unavailable whether emotionally or physically, the teen will not be able to fully develop either. Because our society does not provide enough supports for parents, like affordable childcare or a living wage, or adequate protection for the larger community, like gun control and affordable healthcare, many adults out there are just teenagers in adult bodies, pretending to be adults.

Our Adaptive Teens have internalized how they were parented, so if you were abused, your inner teen will learn to be abusive or to tolerate abuse. If you were gaslit, your inner teen will either gaslight others or Self-gaslight by believing others over yourself. If you were neglected, your inner teen will either be hyper-focused on their own needs or not realize they have any. Specifically, your Adaptive Teen will parent and attempt to control your inner Adaptive Children just as you were controlled or neglected, often retraumatizing your Self and repeating the unresolved trauma of your caregivers.

Personally, my self-worth was contingent on my career success, appearance, pleasing friends, and being in a romantic relationship. Because I had no boundaries, I was needless and wantless in my relationships, and I often tried to anticipate the other person's needs so that I could fulfill them. As a result of not having any of my needs met, I communicated indirectly and with passive aggression, believing that I was the perpetual victim. Not only was I highly critical of others if they didn't appear "proper" or do what the authority wanted, but I was also a perfectionist due to my intense fear of failure and disappointing others.

FOUNDATION OF PSYCHOLOGICAL BOUNDARY FRAMEWORK: RIGHTS OF A CHILD

To recap, young childhood is when each of us begins to determine our sense of Self in the world: wanted or unwanted, good or bad, loved or unloved, safe or unsafe, deserving of protection or completely vulnerable, allowed to have needs and wants or not allowed desires. This Self-concept is foundational to how we develop. Resetting this foundation is required to successfully go through the four-step process I will illustrate in subsequent chapters.

Historically, children have been viewed as property – to be seen and not heard. Spare the rod, spoil the child. I still see adults, myself included, demand that children just follow directions as a sign of respect. For Black and Brown children, there is an additional level of dehumanization.

Contextually, enslaved people were bred like chattel, and those babies subsequently became the property of the enslavers, not children, and definitely not fully human. This mentality of ownership, in which white people can tell those of color what to do and how to behave, has been passed down generationally. Witnessing America actively exploit, threaten, and harm children, especially those who are poor, identify as LGBTQIA+, and / or of color, became normalized in our society. To include one of many examples, the fact that legislators refuse significant gun reform shows children that the adults in charge do not care about their safety.

For a child to be securely rooted in themselves, they need to be shown that they are unconditionally worthy of love, deserving of protection from abuse and neglect, entitled to access emotional and physical support, and able to get their needs met--regardless of behavior, gender, race, class, sexual identity, size, ability, et cetera. This unconditional love is for everyone, which means every single person on this planet is equally worthy of love and has a right to pursue happiness as long as it doesn't harm another who is also deserving to live their life. This one belief, that we are all inherently worthy, begins to free us all from the shackles of our oppressive society.

Only from this point can I walk my clients - and now you - through the steps of my *Psychological Boundary Framework*:

- Step 1: Identify Who's Driving the Bus
- Step 2: Put Your Functional Adult Behind the Wheel
- Step 3: Right-Size Your Self Back into a Healthy Boundary
- Step 4: Use Non-Violent Communication to Connect to Others

Ready? Let's dive in.

4

STEP 1: IDENTIFY WHO'S DRIVING THE BUS

In a society where a medical condition can bankrupt most of us at any moment, we are dysregulated and stressed most of the time. When our brains are constantly scanning the surroundings for threats of mass shootings, we likely react from the survival part of our brain rather than the wiser part of our brain. The fight-flight-freeze-fawn responses reside in the more primitive part of the brain, the limbic system, which focuses on survival. Living your life from your limbic system is exhausting and can lead to chronic illness because our bodies are not meant to constantly produce and absorb the stress hormones cortisol and adrenaline.

The wiser part of our brain is the prefrontal cortex. I describe this region to my clients as the fully resourced Functional Adult part of the brain. If we are not mindfully bringing our bodies and brains to a sense of safety, then we can stay stuck in survival mode without fully realizing it. This mode often feels like you're exhausted all the time, have difficulty with memory and completing tasks, or feel emotionally on edge and can overreact to seemingly small situations. Essentially this response shows that your body is locked in survival mode which directly impacts your perception, often spiraling you deeper into stress. Accessing the full capacity of the prefrontal cortex means much less stress on the body because you are accessing the full resources of the entire body.

In the previous chapter, I explained the concepts of Adaptive Children (from baby to teen) as the survival strategies we adopt if we're developing in less-than-ideal conditions. Adaptive Children live in our limbic system. Functional Adults live in our prefrontal cortex. Combining this Inner Child work with principles from neuroscience, I help my clients imagine that when we are stressed, our internal Adaptive Children take the wheel, not our Functional Adult.

Identifying who is driving our bus is the first step.

Let's go back to Cathy to illustrate this idea. In Cathy's family of origin, the trauma was her mother's emigration from China during the Communist takeover, often euphemistically referred to as the "Cultural Revolution." Cathy's parents were of the educated elite and would be the target of blame if they stayed in China. Furthermore, emigration often required sponsorship from businesses or universities, which were only offered to top performers or the wealthy elite. Remember Resmaa Menakem's words about how trauma decontextualized in a people can look like culture. Possibly, the "culture" of high achievement in Asian students was connected to this circumstance that opened up promising futures in other countries only if they were the best. This need for high achievement by her mother contributed to Cathy's belief that her worth was contingent on people pleasing and high achievement. The issue with people pleasing is that it is impossible to please everyone. Displeasing people was intolerable to Cathy and led to her inability to set boundaries with her children, her husband, and her colleagues at work.

Throughout Cathy's childhood, everyone learned to walk on eggshells to avoid her mother's wrath. The hypervigilance and accommodation to her mother's mood developed an incredible ability in Cathy to track people's discomfort and to prevent any problems by providing the emotional labor of anticipating other people's needs without them even asking. Because Cathy and her sibling were often compared to each other, she learned to feel constantly guilty—guilt if she did poorly, which allowed her brother who was often scapegoated a break from their mother's misplaced disappointment; and guilt if she did well, which put her in good graces with her mother but often resulted in being bullied by her brother. Pitting her and her brother as competitors created an adversarial dynamic, rather than a supportive one. Cathy's nervous system was used to an environment of highly anxious, passive-aggressive hotheads.

For Cathy, her Wounded Baby felt like she needed to justify her existence through achievement. As a result, Cathy was incredibly driven, hard-working, and a perfectionist.

Cathy's Adaptive Child learned to take up very little space by being invisible, overly flexible, and compliant. Since she was not allowed to set any boundaries for herself, or ask for help without being shamed, when Cathy's Adaptive Child is driving the bus, she is walking on eggshells around everyone's needs. She is hyper-focused on pleasing everyone except herself, even at a cost to her mental health and wellbeing.

Cathy's Adaptive Tween felt okay about her appearance - thin and fair-skinned - since this was the ideal where she grew up in Taiwan, but the shock of moving to the US on her own in high school made her Adaptive Teen very insecure. Living in a predominantly white neighborhood, she didn't feel connected to her Asian-American classmates who spoke and moved differently than she was used to. She watched and mimicked her peers, hoping that no one would notice her intense isolation and loneliness of being on her own in a foreign land.

My clients are used to me pausing them frequently in session to reflect, "Who's driving your bus right now?" This is their cue to pause and feel into their body with curiosity. If it's deep insecurity or fear, it's often the Wounded Baby or Adaptive Child. If it's aggression, withdrawal, victimhood, or desire to people please, it's often the Adaptive Tween or Teen.

Think back to the developmental tasks I covered in Chapter 3 and the accompanying adaptive strategies. If you question your worth, it's likely your very young childhood part. If you question how to respond or blame others, then it's likely your older childhood part. The more we practice this exercise, the more adept we become at differentiating between the Wounded Baby, Adaptive Child, Adaptive Tween, and / or Adaptive Teen.

Many times multiple Inner Adaptive Children are fighting over the wheel, which explains the cycle I witnessed at the start of Cathy's sessions, beginning with her Adaptive Teen: "I hate my husband's self-centeredness. He's such an entitled white man who refuses to share the labor. He's worthless. I need to leave and file for a divorce!"

Next, her Adaptive Child takes over the wheel and begs to stay because "There is no perfect relationship out there. What will happen to the kids? How would I do it all on my own? My mom is going to lose face and disown me by having a shameful divorced daughter."

The Adaptive Tween might add that "No one else will want you. You're so disorganized and ugly now. You don't know what you're doing. If you leave, you're going to be alone for the rest of your life."

Back and forth, these parts fight to find the "right decision." Once you identify who's driving the bus, you can take a step back and remember what prompted these existential adaptations and hold yourself in deep compassion. By reparenting that Adaptive Inner Child, you return to the prefrontal cortex (thinking part) so that the Functional Adult can regain the wheel. That reparenting is the next step.

5

STEP 2: PUT YOUR FUNCTIONAL ADULT BEHIND THE WHEEL

The Functional Adult, as I explain to my clients, is the wise loving parent all children need and deserve. Functional Adults know who they are and what they value; they know what they want and what they don't want. It is someone who is embodied and committed to collective freedom and joy. They also value others as equally as they value themselves—protecting others from possible harm and neglect, advocating for others' right to freedom and joy, mutually respecting others, and committing to social justice.

Unlike the Adaptive Teens living in adult bodies, Functional Adults are grounded in a worldview of equality, non-violence, freedom, social responsibility, and interdependence. As I mentioned before, unlike the Adaptive Children, the Functional Adult resides in the fully resourced part of the brain, the prefrontal cortex.

Once I identify which Adaptive Child is driving the bus in Step 1, the next step is to regulate and calm that particular Adaptive Child so that the Functional Adult can take back the wheel. As I've been saying throughout this book, perfection is not the goal here. Be curious. Be playful. Be present to the sensations in your body as you explore the approach I'm teaching here.

MARIA'S STORY

Maria, a thirty-two-year-old transracial adoptee from Guatemala, reached out to work on setting better boundaries with her colleagues and husband. She also wanted to learn how to manage her panic attacks and constant overwhelm more effectively. During the intake, I learned that Maria was adopted as an infant due to a cleft palate. Currently estranged from her adoptive family due to abuse, Maria was miserable in both her social work position and her tumultuous marriage. Despite her active suicidal ideation, Maria was always punctual, impeccably dressed, and often had a stiff smile while describing her perpetual dread.

In the initial intake, I learned that Maria's adoptive family was a very wealthy oil family in Texas. Her adoptive father was often out of town for work and her adoptive mother was often cruel to Maria, making fun of her by using derogatory names about her birth defect and race. In public, Maria was dressed in high-end clothes, bleach blond hair and darker skin, and always looked perfectly happy standing next to her mom, who often bragged to her friends about "saving" Maria from poverty and her daughter's achievements at school. In private, Maria's mom often threatened to deport her if Maria made a mistake, didn't perform a task quickly enough, or showed any feelings besides happiness.

Although she couldn't remember much from her young childhood, she could intuit that she was likely emotionally neglected and abused. She remembers her mother always drinking and needing to clean up the home while her mother was passed out on the floor. While she did well in school, she isolated herself from peers because the unpredictability of kids stressed her out. Instead, she often walked the periphery of the school yard while imagining the life she would have had back in Guatemala. At home, she often roamed the house in an attempt to avoid her mother at all costs.

During middle school, Maria's physical maturation caused her to gain a lot of attention from boys and popularity as a result. She got her period at age eight. Historically, girls of color have been hypersexualized and fetishized, making them prime targets for advances by grown men. Because Maria was emotionally neglected, she ate up the attention and became the leader of the popular girls. Her mother was very vain, so Maria had a lot of practice with clothing and makeup. Internalizing many of the manipulative tactics of her mother, she was able to control the group dynamics easily by covertly spreading rumors and pitting people against each other.

From high school on, Maria earned the highest marks and set her mind on moving as far as she could from her family. She landed in New England, met her husband in college, got married shortly after getting her bachelor's, and eventually became a social worker for the Department of Children and Families. She started seeing me because she was newly pregnant and experiencing panic attacks.

Together, we identified her childhood adaptations by uncovering the belief systems formed in childhood and how they manifested in day-to-day life. Using Maria as an example, I will share what we came up with and how we healed her psychological and emotional boundary.

WHO'S AT THE WHEEL?

If you experience self-loathing, insecurity, or a lack of will to live, chances are a younger part, like your Wounded Baby and/or your Adaptive Child, is driving. This is because your Self concept begins very young. Feelings of overwhelm and panic often originate from this age because young children's nervous systems are not developed enough to regulate without the help of a primary caregiver.

If you often focus externally, like how people perceive you, how others may respond to you, or making the right decision, chances are your Adaptive Tween or Adaptive Teen is behind the wheel. This is because the focus is relational. Common feelings are shame, anxiety, and anger.

MARIA'S WOUNDED BABY

Maria's adoption records don't have much information, except that she was left at the hospital with a cleft palate in need of surgery. Maria internalized that she was defective, ugly and unwanted. Being a mean drunk, her mother reinforced this belief from a young age. Feeling unwanted makes establishing a joyful life very difficult because there is a belief that it's undeserved.

Healing Maria's Wounded Baby

I use guided visualizations in my work because I can often effect more change as I guide the client back in time, accessing memories housed in the brain and body, and then reprocessing them in a healthier way. Since infancy is all preverbal, I invite my clients to sense into their body for possible answers. When guiding Maria to an imaginary hospital in Guatemala, she dreamed up the room where her mother held her, newly born. Functional Adult Maria entered the room to claim her baby self. Neither of us were prepared for her birth mother to be so protective and refuse to hand the baby over to her!

Maria sensed that her birth mother had already made a plan to leave her with a nurse who would help find a wealthy family who could afford the medical expenses required for the surgery. This protective and calculated response was so surprising to Maria, who always imagined being "discarded" due to her cleft palate. It is not unusual for many adoptees to internalize being abandoned due to some form of defect, whether real or imagined. To believe in a defect places a sense of control within a child, and even though that belief is painful, it is often preferred to having no sense of control.

To build trust with Maria's birth mother at this moment in the visualization, she shared that she was Maria as an adult and that her adoptive parents, while wealthy, turned out to be very abusive. Functional Adult Maria was able to imagine hugging her birth mother, acknowledge the poverty that her mother faced that forced this decision to relinquish her baby, and forgave her. On impulse, Maria promised to make a good life for her baby Self. Maria walked out of that hospital with her beautiful baby Self in her arms and an authentic smile on her face.

Once outside the imagined hospital, with eyes still closed in our session, Maria imagined gazing into her baby's eyes and telling her: *You are precious and perfect. I see you and love you. I take full responsibility and promise to build you a good life. You are safe with me. I won't let anyone hurt you. I want you. I cherish you. I promise to love you no matter what.*

For Maria, this guided visualization released a weight in her heart and made her much less bitter and judgmental about others. Maria's meanness, especially toward her husband, was self-protective, hiding her deep insecurity and fear of being abandoned. At the end of session, her face looked different – a brightness in her eyes as if awakened from a long slumber.

MARIA'S ADAPTIVE CHILD

Elementary school was a safer space for Maria. While she was lonely, her tactic of avoiding the kids gave her ample time to daydream. There were a couple of teachers she felt connected to, even though she wasn't comfortable sharing the truth about her family.

For Maria, her Adaptive Child took up very little space because she believed she didn't deserve it. She learned that making mistakes was dangerous and threatened rejection, even deportation. Because Maria didn't realize that she could set boundaries for herself, relationships felt scary. Maria learned to tolerate loneliness, neglecting her basic needs of affection and connection.

Healing Maria's Adaptive Child

I often guide clients to ask for consent to hold their young child self, especially if there is a history of abuse. In Maria's case, the person who was meant to protect her, Maria's adoptive mom, was the same person who caused her the most pain. I guided Maria to locate her Adaptive Child in the room. She was huddled in a corner looking down. Maria imagined sitting a good distance apart, which allowed me to suggest ways to attune: *Hi, sweetheart. I'm you as a grown up. I'm here to take care of you now. I'm so sorry Mom didn't take care of you like she was supposed to. And that Dad was never there to protect you. That was scary and confusing. You tried so hard to make Mom happy. She was unhappy because Dad was having an affair, so mom took it out on you. It was not ok. It's safe to come out from that corner now. I will not let anyone hurt you or threaten to deport you. Only look to me now for your love and affirma-*

tion. I promise to have your back no matter what. You don't have to pretend to be happy anymore. I will accept however you feel. You belong here with me. I love you no matter what.

By the end, her Adaptive Child was in her lap allowing Maria to hold her. Maria noted that her Adaptive Child was still cautious, which made sense. Trust takes time to build. The more Maria is able to be gentle on herself when she makes mistakes and visualize comforting her Adaptive Child, the more Maria will be able to heal and connect to what brings her joy.

MARIA'S ADAPTIVE TWEEN

Experiencing power for the first time, Maria abused it like her mother did. Her Adaptive Tween became hyper fixated on her appearance and managing her weight in order to be perceived as desirable. She disregarded other people's boundaries just like hers were ignored. She gained pleasure when people felt worse than she did. Although she had a lot of attention due to her appearance, Maria always acted disinterested because internally she was terrified of being vulnerable with anyone. Her mother often said nice things to people's faces and then made fun of them behind their back. As a result, Maria was paranoid and could not trust anyone to be honest with her.

Healing Maria's Adaptive Tween

The Adaptive Tween needs to know that there is nothing wrong with them and that they are accepted, loved, and cherished for who they are—a perfectly imperfect human whose back you'll always have, even when they are held accountable for any harm they inevitably commit.

Imagining her Adaptive Tween, Maria saw her with a full face of makeup trying to act confident, while her eyes darted back and forth, scanning for risks. Maria imagined herself gently putting her hands on Maria's Adaptive Tween shoulders: *I see you. You were born with a cleft palate but that doesn't make you defective. I know how scared you are to be hurt. It's ok. I'm here now. I will protect you. I will remind you how special you are and perfect. No matter how you look or what you say, you are no better or worse than anyone else. You don't have to warp the truth to avoid getting in trouble. Only look to me for your love and assurance. No one else. I will have your back even when you make mistakes. You're behaving so meanly because that's what you learned from Mom. It doesn't make you bad. And it's not ok. It feels good in the moment to be mean but you stay so lonely. You deserve to feel close to people. Your birth mother wants you to have a good life. Thank you for adapting this way to try and protect us. But I'm here now and will protect you. Let me take the wheel.*

Take as long as you need to trust me. I will never abandon you because I love you.

MARIA'S ADAPTIVE TEEN

Adaptive Teens internalize how they were parented. Maria's Adaptive Teen is hypercritical of others, feels entitled to special treatment to make up for her abuse, and uses threats and manipulation to get what she wants. This is particularly the case with her husband, who is often emotionally unavailable. When Maria lashes out, he responds by belittling her and threatening divorce, which is his own Adaptive Teen.

Healing Maria's Adaptive Teen

Adaptive teenagers need the following: respect for who they are and how they adapted, validation for their viewpoint and feelings, and then for the Functional Adult to set a firm and appropriate boundary. Maria imagines leaning to the side to bump shoulders with her Adaptive Teenager, who sits next to her:

Thank you so much for all the ways you adapted in order to get us here. It is because of your resourcefulness and resilience that we survived Mom. I am so proud of you, your strength, and your hard work. I owe everything to you. Thank you. I completely understand why you behaved the way you did. Needing to be perfect in order to be perceived a certain way. Needing others to be perfect to demonstrate they were trustworthy and loved you. It makes sense. But I'm here now, your Functional Adult. I am the one that you've been waiting for. Not your husband, not your job, not your parents, and not this baby. I'm here now. I see and value you, and have your back no matter what. And I need you to let me drive the bus from now on. That means I need you to stop trying to control our younger Adaptive Children, too. I know you mean well, but it's not helping anymore. The ways you were parented are not the ways that you all need. Let me take care of them now, too. I appreciate you for all you've done. I will take the wheel now. I'm so proud of you and will never abandon you or your needs ever again. I'm sorry it's taken me this long, but I'm here now and I'm ready to build the life you deserve. I'm ready to do it imperfectly, compassionately, and from now on. Only look to me for your love and validation, no one and nothing else.

PRACTICE MAKES PROGRESS

Just like teenagers need to get a learner's permit before they earn their driver's license, our Functional Adults need to practice regaining the wheel over and over again. Our nervous systems need to learn a new way of being. That takes time, repetition, and compassion for the mistakes that will be made and corrected with loving accountability for any harm committed.

As I tell all my clients, if the emotional response is intense, then it is ten percent present moment and ninety percent from the past. In other words, "Hysterical is historical." Childhood trauma by its very nature occurs in a time of powerlessness, which means a child needs a compassionate adult to help them process their feelings and experiences. As a result, if the trauma or belief has not been processed and resolved appropriately, the brain will actively, albeit unconsciously, look for people and situations to provide another chance to resolve and heal the original wound. For example, my clients who grew up in a violent home, like Maria, will be drawn to relationships that are domestically violent or emotionally manipulative. The sensation of being unsafe, while painful, is the situation that feels familiar and comfortable because their nervous system knows what to expect and what to do in that situation. So normalize and anticipate that your Functional Adult will not be perfect. Remember, perfection is not the goal. Authenticity, embodiment, compassionate accountability, and living freely alongside others, taking care of each other interdependently are the goals.

Another benefit of this approach is that you begin seeing who's driving other people's proverbial buses, too. Maria's husband grew up wealthy yet emotionally neglected because he was essentially raised by nannies. Maria healing her boundaries by reparenting her inner Adaptive Children allows her to relate to her husband from her own Functional Adult—inviting his Functional Adult to show up. Specifically, as Maria practiced this new way of approaching her life, she learned to regulate herself into her Functional Adult—her prefrontal, fully resourced part of her brain—so that she could speak more directly and with more vulnerability to her husband. That allowed her husband to see her authenticity, feel emotionally connected to someone he loved, and hear her behavioral requests rather than the complaints and manipulation from her Adaptive T/ween.

My clients know that they don't need the other person to be regulated to their Functional Adult to transform their lives. From our coaching sessions, Cathy, like Maria, learned to develop her newly discovered Functional Adult such that she also understands how to strategically communicate with David based on who she thinks is driving his bus. She can do this without taking on the inappropriate emotional labor of being his caretaker. That emotional care needs to come from David's own Functional Adult, and whether or not he chooses to access this way of relating to her will inform Cathy of next steps in their marriage. The same goes for Maria.

This internal shift from the Adaptive Children

driving the bus to our Functional Adult also positively impacts every aspect of our lives. For Maria, her relationship to work changed. She is learning to relate to her social work clients as people doing the best they can with what they have – experts in their own lives whom she is there to journey with, rather than to save. Her burnout is shifting now that she is centering her own needs and exploring what brings her joy.

With Maria's friendships, she's learning whom she can really trust by showing authentic parts of her Self and seeing how those parts are received. The friends' responses do not determine her value, like they did in the past. Instead, their responses inform Maria's next boundary—whether or not to become a bit more porous to allow friends to be more emotionally intimate with her, or to be more rigid and create more distance.

Keep these terms - "porous" and "rigid" - in mind because differentiating between the two is critical to understanding the next steps in my *Psychological Boundaries Framework.*

6

STEP 3: RIGHT-SIZE YOUR SELF BACK INTO A HEALTHY BOUNDARY

Now that you know that there is nothing inherently wrong with you—that your body is responding to beliefs you created in childhood and were reinforced in your environment—you will have a clearer understanding of how to relate from a psychological boundary grounded in equality, non-violence, freedom, social responsibility, and interdependence.

Healthy boundaries are when you experience your Self as equal to and as precious as another. You and everyone else are inherently worthy and special – no more and no less than another. Everyone has a right to express themselves and pursue their life as they want as long as it does not infringe on the same rights of another human being.

Healthy boundaries are also about sharing your

experience in appropriate ways that do not over-burden or disregard the other person. Picture this: healthy boundaries are a Venn diagram where you are one circle, responsible for regulating your emotions, setting boundaries, and advocating for your needs and wants in a respectful way. The second circle is the other person who is also responsible for regulating their emotions, setting boundaries, and respectfully advocating for their needs and wants in a respectful way. When you interact with another person, the shared space between the circles, overlapping as in a Venn diagram, is the collaborative problem solving needed to negotiate shared goals and desires.

This collaborative problem solving looks different depending on the people involved: Self and partner, Self and child, Self and person with more authority, and Self and person with less authority. Within these different contexts, I refer again to Cathy's story as well as give examples from my own life so you can see how the *Psychological Boundaries Framework* worked for her and may begin to imagine how it might work for you.

SELF + PARTNER DYNAMIC AS EQUALS, EACH RESPONSIBLE FOR SHOWING UP AS FUNCTIONAL ADULTS

Through Cathy's boundary healing, she has gradually been improving her relationship with David. As she builds empathy and compassion for her internal Adaptive Children, naturally she is able to hold more empathy and compassion for David without falling into the patriarchal trap of taking care of him by centering his needs above her own. David is responsible for reparenting his own Adaptive Children – whether or not he is aware of them. His choice of how he shows up in their relationship informs her next boundaries with him: get emotionally closer or more distant.

Now, Cathy is better able to regulate herself back to and live from her Functional Adult. She right-sizes herself to be bigger to take up more space in the family by prioritizing her needs, setting firm boundaries, and expressing clear expectations with her children and David. At the same time, Cathy knows how to right-size David's learned entitlement without shaming him. Her learning to tolerate her husband's discomfort in being right-sized down allows David to practice tolerating it himself.

Understanding David's trauma around being emotionally neglected due to his mother's unhealed grief about his sister's stillbirth has allowed Cathy to hold his reactivity with compassion while being firm about how he needs to step up into his roles as co-parent to their children and equal partner to her.

A big insight for her was that when David expresses annoyance, Cathy used to take his sigh as the final decision: "No, I don't want to." Being raised to obey authority without question contributed to the power imbalance within their relationship. Now, Cathy understands that David's responses do not reflect his goodness, nor her lovability. His response is merely the start of the conversation. Together, they carefully navigate through conflict to get to an outcome that meets both of their needs. Again, David's responses inform her next boundary—whether to continue to open up and deepen their emotional intimacy by sharing her internal process or to close her boundary to protect herself and her children from prioritizing his needs over theirs. From that place, Cathy is now able to make better informed decisions on her next steps within her relationship.

SELF + CHILD DYNAMIC WITH VARYING NEEDS, RESPONSIBILITIES, AND POWER

Young Children

With Cathy and her young children, she now understands that at those ages, her kids are completely dependent on her and her husband. As the adults in the relationship, their kids rely on them, their parents with fully developed brains, to attune to what they might need and want, and help them feel safe and seen even though they might not always be pleased by their parents' responses and boundaries.

If Cathy continues to be reactive and condescending to Daniel, he may learn to see himself as annoying and stupid, which will impact not only his psychological boundary, but also how he shows up in the world and treats others. For example, if Daniel internalizes that he cannot please his mother, he might internalize being bad or incompetent, which might make him have a chip on his shoulder by being reactive and condescending to others in order to protect his fragile ego.

Cathy's big insight around her children was that their emotional expression and verbalization of their desires triggered the Adaptive Child in her who learned to stop showing up. Now, as she is physically affectionate with her children, and more tolerant of their messiness and imperfection, she can imagine her own Adaptive Child joyfully playing alongside her own children. That Adaptive Child can experience Functional Adult Cathy looking at her with pride and unconditional love, reliving a childhood she never experienced.

We also talked about the start of racial identity development at this point in her children's lives. She knows that she and her husband need to have those conversations about race and racism now so that her children can manage these complicated conversations when they face racism and bias on their own. What Cathy and I deduced during our work together was that Daniel was being mistreated by some peers due to being biracial, particularly half-Chinese.

The COVID-19 pandemic increased anti-Asian hate over 300 percent. Cathy's racial identity development was different as she was surrounded by other Asian bodies growing up in Taiwan. This is in stark contrast to Daniel's growing up as a minority within a predominantly white community in the United States, a country built on the history of white supremacy and the cruel enslavement of Africans that enabled capitalism.

Once Cathy realized that his peers were accusing

him of having Covid and influencing classmates to avoid him, I could coach her to leverage David's white male privilege to contact the teacher and principal, copying Cathy on the email, to report and address this issue. As peer dynamics improved for Daniel, so did his behaviors at home and relationship with his mother.

Children are at the mercy of those in authority. Believing at your core that there is nothing wrong with your child, and that they may need a different way of responding or additional support, will help you provide the environment in which your child needs to thrive. Your leadership, compassion, imperfect modeling, and unconditional love (for them and your Self) will help them understand their own preciousness while also learning to respect and cherish others as equally precious and deserving of protection.

Tweens

With tweens, as they go through puberty and make lots of impulsive decisions that inevitably harm themselves or someone else, they need your guidance to process the outcome of their decisions so they can understand what happened, hold themselves with compassionate accountability, and internalize the growth. At this stage of development, your tween needs lots of space and clear boundaries to explore their interests and learn who they are and how they identify themselves so that they can naturally attract peers who will accept and cherish them. They will also need your modeling on how to protect themselves.

My older daughter is at this tween stage. She's on a soccer team that brings in young adult soccer coaches from Europe to help enrich the soccer program. One particular guest coach was an attractive young man in his early to mid-twenties. Notably, many of the tween girls were awkwardly silly and openly flirted with him. After that particular practice, I spoke with my daughter and some of her teammates, normalizing any crushes they might have, since puberty increases a sense of romantic attraction. I emphasized that this is the time to explore what qualities they might find attractive, and so forth with peers. I also made a point to talk about how it would never be appropriate for a man the coach's age or in his position of power to make any romantic advances towards them, even if they flirted in the first place. Together we identified concrete steps to take if it ever happened. Though talking about sexuality can be uncomfortable for some parents, I prefer to err on the side of too many conversations about safety, especially around their bodies, than not enough.

The most recent statistics in 2023 report that one in nine girls experiences sexual abuse from an adult before age 18. Unfortunately, I was one of those girls. The power dynamic between me and the adult male perpetrator, a high school teacher, made it impossible for me to come forward, especially since my mother likely would have blamed me, an outcome many women and girls experience firsthand.

Conversations between tweens and caregivers are not the only factor that will help tweens navigate this stage of development. Finding a peer group where your tween can be authentic will also serve them well. I often work with people who feel lonely within groups of friends because they never uncovered their authentic Self. Instead, many tweens, especially those who are on social media, learn to focus on how to be liked and accepted within the status quo rather than practice being true to oneself and learning to tolerate rejection as they find them Selves and the friends with whom they can be authentic and vulnerable.

Teens

With your teen, this is the time to support them to go out and practice adulting, as they hopefully have internalized the values and boundaries you've taught them.

In the cases of Cathy, Maria, and myself we ventured out alone as adults at sixteen. It was too soon and with too little support. Focusing on Cathy here, she was sent to the United States to live in an apartment alone in high school. On the surface, Cathy performed well, but the expectation that a sixteen-year-old is mature enough to be adulting on their own is misguided. Cathy was profoundly lonely, extremely anxious, and lucky enough to have avoided crossing paths with anyone who would have taken advantage of her situation. Instead, Cathy put on a mask by emulating the behaviors and goals of the peers around her. Rather than processing experiences with her mother in China over the phone, Cathy omitted her mistakes and confusion to avoid being shamed and blamed. Instead, Cathy internalized that she was incompetent and needed to hide it from others, especially her mother. When she began dating David, her Adaptive Teen was relieved to just follow his dreams and pursuits, rather than discover her own. There was no way for her to know what that decision would cost her in the long run. And our coaching space was where she practiced gathering data on the outcomes so that she could regain control of the rest of her journey.

Teens and young adults need more than just financial support. They need unconditional love, the freedom and respect to make their own choices, and the space and emotional support to collect data on the outcome of those choices. Discerning whether or not to continue down a particular path helps them to slowly build a life they *want* to live, rather than a life they think they're supposed to create.

As the parent, even though you may be white knuckling this experience, your respect for your young adult as a unique whole person will help them stay aligned to who they are as they meet and work for other adults who will treat them differently from you. Your trust in them to find their own way while providing your unconditional support (not to be confused with bailing them out or controlling their decisions) teaches them that they can trust themselves and are allowed and expected to advocate for their needs and wants in a respectful non-violent way with everyone they encounter. Your respectful and compassionate responses when they inevitably make mistakes model how to be held accountable for harm, and how to hold others accountable when they themselves are inevitably harmed. Tolerating your young adult's emotional distress will allow them to mature, with continued practice, into a Functional Adult.

Have you noticed that I refer to harming others and being harmed by others as inevitable? I want to be clear about the distinction between emotional and physical harm. Emotional harm is part of developing intimacy with others. As different individuals, we will inevitably cross other people's boundaries without realizing it. That harm should be acknowledged, processed, and repaired with full accountability, and without shame or blame. Physical harm due to neglect or abuse, however, is *not* to be tolerated. For example, the fact that the United States has learned to tolerate gun violence by prioritizing the rights of gun owners over the rights of individuals to live safe from harm is neither healthy nor appropriate. So for young teachers, new to the field, we as a society are failing to model the protection and support they need as individuals charged with protecting younger more vulnerable children.

SELF + AUTHORITY DYNAMIC WITH VARYING ACCESS TO POWER

Cathy now understands that her firm, dominated by older white men, is a hostile work environment for her as an Asian-American woman. Remember that a key part of the *Psychological Boundaries Framework* is acknowledging the larger societal contexts that we are in. For Cathy, this process meant learning about the model minority myth as well as her internalized misogyny and anti-Blackness. Empowering herself with this knowledge has allowed a clarity within her on how to protect her psychological and emotional boundary while strategically advocating for her needs.

Cathy was surprised that her improved self-esteem by right-sizing her Self at work meant that she no longer needed to overcompensate by overworking. Approaching her colleagues as equals, which involved right-sizing them down in her mind, has resulted in better working relationships with some of her colleagues who were also feeling insecure. With those colleagues, Cathy will strengthen those connections so they can have her back in meetings.

Unfortunately, healing boundaries will also show whom you cannot trust. As Cathy increased her confidence by setting firmer boundaries, her director manager increased his belligerence, and now she knows she will need more rigid boundaries with him. To maintain those boundaries, Cathy decided to speak only about concrete tasks with him rather than engage on topics of performance or comparison of her and her peers.

Using this workplace as "research," Cathy created a checklist of the environment in which she thrives so that she could begin her new job search. The constant gaslighting, microaggressions, and condescension at work drained her of so much energy that it made it impossible to be joyful at home. By focusing on building the life that best suited her and her desires for her family, she started taking steps to create her own company where she will invest in women-led startups. Cathy realized that she often worked in settings where her boss was never satisfied with her. While difficult, this was a very familiar experience for her because she learned this dynamic in childhood. Creating a new business with her husband's emotional and financial support has re-engaged both of them as equal partners.

SELF + DIRECT REPORT DYNAMIC WITH VARYING ACCESS TO POWER

For Sue, another client I have in middle management, this self + direct report dynamic was really interesting. Sue is a Black woman from Arkansas who moved to Boston for graduate school. Even though she attended a prestigious university to earn her master's degree in public health, she was riddled with insecurity and feelings of being a fraud. This is a common occurrence for students of color attending prestigious universities. The subtle cues and microaggressions often make students of color feel unwelcome, belittled, and paranoid. With Sue, we needed to contextualize her graduate experience. The prestigious and elite institution had a history of being exclusively for white men until Affirmative Action was put in place, which reluctantly forced the institution's admission process to open up to qualified candidates of more diverse backgrounds, which included white women and students of color.

Sue recently earned a promotion and managed a team of home health aide workers. With me, she wanted to address symptoms of depression and some challenges she was having at work. My conversations with her revealed that while Sue grew up with a solid sense of her Black-American identity, she learned to shrink herself down to accommodate the comfort of her white teachers and peers. When she attended this elite institution for a career about which she felt passionate, the professors' feedback and subtle microaggressions slowly and seamlessly eroded her confidence. At the clinic she managed, Sue was often undermined by the white office administrator and felt like she needed to walk on eggshells to avoid being misunderstood. She often felt stuck between trying to get the people she managed to like her and needing to constantly prove herself to upper management.

One coaching session in particular resonated in my mind. In speaking about a colleague who needed to work from home while her child was sick, she rattled off, "I need to make sure the nurse doesn't take advantage of the system." We paused and identified her people pleasing Adaptive Teen driving the bus trying to be a respected manager. Also fighting for the wheel was her Adaptive Child who longed to be accepted by her peers. Context is key as well: a couple of nurse practitioners were Nigerian, and while Sue and these Nigerian colleagues shared a similar skin tone, Sue sensed some judgment from them. Since the nurse practitioners had grown up as part of the dominant culture in Nigeria, they had not experienced the relentlessness of institutionalized racism and perpetual white violence and neglect in America. It made sense to Sue that this animosity between Africans and Black Americans stemmed from the way that Black Americans or African-Americans are portrayed in global media, which is intentionally skewed.

Sue's insecurities from her Adaptive Child and Adaptive Tween about being smart enough and accepted by white peers and teachers were triggered by her Nigerian direct reports and her white American upper management's internalized anti-Blackness.

I explained to Sue that there would rarely, if ever, be a time that an individual will abuse the system, like how the system abuses individuals. The system is intentionally set up to prioritize profit over people. As a manager, who needs to have healthy psychological boundaries, she needed to advocate for her direct reports so that they had adequate support and reasonable and humane expectations for their job. This job was not their life; this job funded their life.

I also encouraged her to address behavior, not

attack character. Her colleague's child was sick, and she did not have family here to help with childcare. I wanted her to see that when you align yourself with the role of empowering your staff and having their backs while holding them accountable for missed tasks, you will see if your managers will support you in treating them as human. That information from your managers will show you if this is an environment in which you can thrive.

Lastly, I reminded Sue that she did not need to prove herself to anyone. She needed to right-size her Self smaller from the Adaptive Teen who wanted to show her direct report who's boss. At the same time, she needed to right-size her Self bigger from the Adaptive Child and Adaptive Tween so she knows that as she is, she is enough. She was not their friend. She did not need their acceptance to be deemed valuable. Her role was to protect them from being exploited by the system so that they knew she had their backs. She could do this work of staying in her lane by maintaining a healthy psychological boundary. Take their responses as data about them, and how much energy to invest at a job that funds her life. None of this was about her.

Right-sizing others needs to be coupled with practicing non-violent communication to ensure that your words match your behaviors. Non-violent communication, developed by the late Dr. Marshall B. Rosenberg, is such a valuable tool. Its premise is that everyone is just trying to get needs met. When you listen for their needs, rather than as an attack, you are able to communicate non-violently. This is the next and final step in my *Psychological Boundaries Framework*.

STEP 4: USE NON-VIOLENT COMMUNICATION TO CONNECT TO OTHERS

The reason why we need to use non-violent communication is so we stop the cycle of violence, supremacy, and oppression. When trauma is unprocessed, our brains and body unknowingly hyperfocus on it in order to avoid it from happening again. That unintentional focus to avoid it actually brings it front and center in our psyche. That is why reparenting our inner Adaptive Children will finally heal the root of the hurt so that we can stop passing on the generational harm by continuing to oppress and harm others.

For us to decolonize ourselves and our relationships, we need our internal and external communication to be direct, compassionate, and focused on behaviors. We communicate our internal experience to be known, not to be right nor to be better than someone else.

The steps are incredibly simple, structured, and powerful. It's important to understand that everyone has their own worldviews, like glasses, from which they experience and perceive reality. The Feedback Wheel that I'm about to explain allows you to let someone else see into your personal experience that you own one hundred percent.

But first, let's return to Cathy. One of Cathy's goals was to improve her communication with her husband. The way we worked on that was to practice non-violent communication. Non-violent communication helps you to identify your own needs and listen empathically for the needs of others. It breaks down the art of communicating so that the speaker takes full responsibility for their own feelings rather than place blame on any other person.

The non-violent communication structure I use is to first identify the behavior or language.

Most clients roll their eyes when I teach them how to use non-violent communication, but then they are so grateful once they understand how useful it can be in feeling closer with their partners. Communicating in this way is not only effective, but also compassionate. Many clients have praised this skill acquisition because they use it in all aspects of their life now. Non-violent communication can de-escalate tense situations, get people to see eye to eye even if they don't agree, and help you feel seen.

The basic premise of using non-violent communication is to communicate observations, feelings, needs, and requests peacefully and respectfully with others. Another way to understand it is that you are inviting the other person to see you authentically.

Here are the rules:

1. Everyone is inherently worthy.
2. Assume good intentions. This keeps you out of defensiveness.
3. Listen with curiosity, like a journalist, not a lawyer.
4. Use "I statements." Speaking from your truth helps prevent you from crossing someone else's emotional or psychological boundaries.
5. State specific behavioral requests, rather than criticizing or complaining. This allows the other person an opportunity to know what you are asking for and can then choose whether or not they do it.
6. Share to be known, not to be right.
7. Use the Feedback Wheel.

The *Feedback Wheel* is structured into four parts:

A. Name the observational data.
B. Share your interpretation of the data.
C. Identify the feeling that results from your interpretation.
D. State a specific behavioral request.

Here's how it looks put together: *When you* [A-Observational data], *the story I make up is* [B-Interpretation]. *That story makes me feel* [C-Emotion]. *Can you* [D-Behavioral request]?

For people who were not afforded a lot of space or authority over their lives, requests can be perceived as demands. Healing your boundary will include relearning how to communicate and hear the experience of the other person as real and as valid as your own experience. Negotiations need not be a win-lose dynamic. Requests become the start of conversations where you and the other person's needs are centered equally.

Let's return to Cathy's situation to see what this looked like in practice.

USING THE FEEDBACK WHEEL

Along with guided visualizations, I provide opportunities to role play in order to practice using the tools

I teach. Role-playing as Cathy I said, "David, when you skip the kids' swim class without telling me, the story I make up is that you are prioritizing your rest over the labor of bringing the kids to swim class. That story makes me feel angry and sad. Can you tell me why you decided not to go and not tell me ahead of time?"

In the role of David, Cathy developed some empathy for her husband. She realized that her questioning of his decision-making played into the bias that men didn't know how to properly parent. And that Cathy's anxiety to make the perfect decision often triggered her husband's insecurity about disappointing her, resulting in him emotionally withdrawing or becoming defensive.

Let's take a step back here to reflect on the conversation. Cathy's task is to use the non-violent communication skills to share her experience with David in a non-violent way and make behavioral requests. With a bit of guidance, she determined that email correspondence is best as she tends to track his facial expressions, which influences what she shares and how she shares it in the moment. Here's where we landed for the email:

"David, I have something important to share. Please read this so that we can talk about it tonight after the kids go to bed. I really appreciate how hard you work for the family. You are such a dedicated husband and father. When I tell you the family plan and you roll your eyes and sigh, the story I make up is that you don't like spending time with me or the kids. That story reminds me of how I felt like a burden and an annoyance to my mom when I was a child, and that story makes me feel sad, lonely, and frustrated. Do you want to go with us to the zoo, or would you rather have some time alone? If you go with us to the zoo and are distracted by work, I will be annoyed and would rather you not go. If I go on my own to the zoo, I will need three hours to myself when I get back, so you would be in charge of attending to our children. What works for you?

"Sweetheart, when I see you so stressed about work, the story I make up is that you don't see how much we miss you and want to spend time with you. Are you okay? I notice that your mood has gotten worse lately. Does this have to do with your dad's death anniversary coming up? Is there anything I can do to support you?"

David's response will inform her next boundary. The start of this email invites his Functional Adult by stating her appreciation of him as a person and equal partner. Then she uses the Feedback Wheel to show her internal experience to David. She is sharing to be known, not to be right. Next, her behavioral request is about the plans: will you go with us to the zoo or not? She states clearly the consequences of his decisions. These are not threats; Cathy is providing information for David to digest so that he doesn't have to mindread. This information allows David to make an informed decision.

Mind reading is a trauma reaction. No one is able to read anyone's mind. To expect it means you are in one of your inner Adaptive Children.

The last paragraph in the email is an invitation for emotional connection and intimacy. If he shames her or accuses her of being crazy, then she knows to pull away and have more of a rigid boundary. If he withdraws and is unwilling to engage or talk about his feelings, she will then talk about the impact on her because she needs emotional intimacy in her marriage to feel safe and seen. These steps gradually keep both informed on if they grow together or if they grow apart. Neither direction is good or bad. It is honest. Cathy needs to get clear on if David is willing to do his own emotional labor because it is not appropriate for partners to be the other person's primary emotional caretaker, like a parent to a child. That is co-dependence rather than the goal of interdependence.

Co-dependence means that my value is dependent on some other thing outside of myself like saving someone from their emotional pain, or needing to work more than what is necessary, or needing someone else's approval or love. Our society not only sanctions co-dependence, but promotes it in order to center a culture of consumption.

Since the focus of these conversations that use non-violent communication is to connect and hear each other's experiences and needs, there are no losers. How the other person responds to your non-violence is data about how close you can get to that person or if you need to create more distance.

If there is nothing wrong with you and there is nothing wrong with the other person, then you are listening for what is needed in the environment to create enough space and safety so the needs of all those involved are met.

Now that you've learned the four steps of the *Psychological Boundary Framework*, let's talk more about translating theory into practice. In the next chapter, I invite you to walk the talk, or drive the bus, and embody the teachings from the previous chapters.

BOUNDARIES: PUTTING IT ALL TOGETHER

What I've noticed in myself and those I work with is that setting boundaries theoretically feels very different from when we *embody* boundaries. In other words, talking about *how* to set boundaries is not the same as understanding how boundaries impact how you see your sense of Self, and subsequently, how you move in the world.

Let's make sure we are all on the same page: Psychological and emotional boundaries are where I end and where another person begins. I describe boundaries like a bubble around each person. Within that bubble, I am in charge of determining my identity, identifying what I want and don't want, what I like and don't like. As an adult, I am also in charge of protecting myself physically and emotionally from other people, and protecting other people from myself so that boundaries are not crossed without consent. Additionally, each person is in charge of regulating their own emotions and communicating in a way that is non-violent to themselves and others.

Boundaries are difficult to embody because our society historically not only models dysfunctional boundaries, but actually discourages healthy boundaries. Praising the martyrdom of mothers leads to burnout as a badge of honor. Toxic masculinity socializes men to be disconnected from their emotions and shames men for any feelings of vulnerability as a human experience. People see their value based on productivity rather than inherent. Moreover, many social norms promote co-dependence as the goal: When you get married, then you are whole. If you find a partner who wants you, only then are you worthy. Only when your body looks a certain way are you considered and permitted to feel beautiful. Achieving a certain level of prestige and wealth determines success. It is no wonder that so many people are so stressed out. The standard of living is not only unattainable for the majority of us; it is lethal.

From the highest authority, our government protects people unequally. Specifically, women are now no longer allowed full body autonomy. In many states, parents are no longer allowed to provide gender affirming care for their trans children. Historically, people have had to fight to gain equal rights: the right to vote for Black people, women, and immigrants of color; the right to access buildings and transportation for those who are disabled; and the right to marriage for those of the same gender.

Unequal access to resources, support, and protection is like inhaling carbon monoxide – it kills each of us slowly and invisibly. Subtle and not-so-subtle messages communicate expectations that fuel the low-grade misery that a majority of our population suffer from, as indicated by the astronomical numbers of people taking anti-depressants and anti-anxiety medication. If so many people need medication to get through the day, then we should start looking at what is expected of us and makes us mentally ill.

THE CONCEPT OF PSYCHOLOGICAL BOUNDARIES

The way I illustrate Psychological Boundaries with my clients is by using circles cut out of fabric that represent how much space someone is allowed to take up in our society compared to someone else in the same situation.

The *small circle* represents someone who is invisible like those who are poor, chronically ill, immigrants, uneducated, non-English speaking,

LGBTQIA+, non-Christian, or those of darker pigment, larger size, or "alternative" family structures.

The *medium circle* represents equal size to others, symbolizing the foundational belief that every single human is unconditionally loveable. This equal-to-everyone size is the goal of boundary healing work, where we "right size" each person as equal and worthy of love, protection, accountability, and freedom to pursue their life.

The *large circle* represents someone who is historically centered, like white cis-gender heterosexual men. Historical narratives portray them in a positive light, elevated above others. These people are entitled to more freedom, power, and privilege and are immediately assumed to be right, smarter, more skilled, and more deserving of their ease and comfort.

Within a relational dynamic, the size of the circle can change depending on the environment, which I will illustrate with a case study about a couple named Darryl and Gretchen. Darryl, a Black cis-man, will historically have more privilege when discussing household duties with his wife Gretchen, a white bisexual cis-woman, due to the impact of patriarchy. When following their conversation, I hold up the circles to represent power dynamics within the relationship. As emotions come into the conversation, the circle sizes change quickly due to generational trauma, like patriarchy and racialized trauma. When Gretchen becomes tearful about how Darryl expresses his frustration about her passive aggression around doing the dishes, Darryl's larger circle from patriarchal privilege rapidly shrinks down to the smaller circle due to the impact of white body supremacy and the very real risk of white women's tears.

Being able to name the power dynamics using the circles creates a concrete way to visualize who is "allowed" more space or privilege around a certain issue, which then gives us a concrete way to name the societal context and a path to right size both of them.

Using the above example, here's how I coached Darryl and Gretchen through the negotiation of division of household labor. I first named the context and impact of patriarchy on their relationship: "Both of you were taught the assumed invisible emotional undervalued labor of women. Gretchen, you have the practiced skill of multitasking and have received praise for emotionally taking care of others. You need to right-size your circle up by reminding yourself that your value is not dependent on how your house looks and how little you inconvenience your husband with your needs. Darryl, you have the hidden expectation that your partner will communicate to you what needs to be done so you can happily do it. That expectation puts an additional level of responsibility on Gretchen to project manage the household duties, which is unfair and inappropriate. Darryl, you need to right-size your circle down to look at the house and identify different tasks you can take on proactively, without then needing praise that it was done."

Then I named the context and impact of racism on their relationship: "Both of you have internalized the harm of colorism. Darryl, when you see Gretchen cry about how you voice your frustration, your body perceives her as another fragile white woman that you've had to learn to defer and submit to your whole life in order to stay safe. Expand your circle back to the right size by reminding yourself that you are safe here and you have the same right to claim your needs as Gretchen does. You carefully picked a partner committed to being anti-racist, so continue voicing your request for her to clarify her needs while listening to Gretchen's behavioral request. Her request is the start of the conversation, not a demand you need to complete. You are safe in this relationship, and you are not bad for not pleasing your partner. She's responsible for making herself happy."

We then continued: "Gretchen, when you hear Darryl's frustration, you get triggered back to how your parents centered your father's stress around work as the primary breadwinner, so you learned to avoid asking for your needs directly in case it would upset your dad. Rather than your learned passive aggression around asking for what you need, allow yourself to take up equal space. Your needs are as important as his. Remember, Darryl is responsible to take care of his frustration, not you. You carefully picked your husband because of his commitment to building an equal partnership. It is safe to ask for your needs early, clearly and often, before you need to collapse into blame and shame for either upsetting Darryl or not feeling seen. Move to right-size and name your concrete behavioral requests, which is the start of the conversation, not the demand. No one's needs are more important than another's."

INTERNAL EMOTIONAL BOUNDARIES

These same circles are also used to represent the internal emotional boundaries of my clients that are largely influenced by our Inner Adaptive Children and how that part perceives the world. Asking my clients "Who's driving the bus right now?" helps them pause to consider if their Adaptive Child, Adaptive Tween, or Adaptive Teen is at the wheel. Determining who is driving helps them understand how to regulate themselves back into the right-size. In other words, when we realize that we are experiencing the situation from an Adaptive Child perspective that resides in the survival part of the brain (limbic system), that cues us to regulate ourselves into our thinking part of the brain (prefrontal cortex), where I imagine our Functional Adult resides. If you are feeling exhausted or burned out, you are likely living from your Adaptive Children whereas Functional Adults have access to the full resources of the brain and tend to feel more energized and inspired.

For the internal emotional boundary, the *small circle* represents the Wounded Baby, the Adaptive Child, and sometimes the Adaptive Tween because they've internalized that their worth is conditional. The Wounded Baby often perceives that their existence is either unwanted or burdensome. This can sometimes manifest behaviorally as an unwillingness to fully claim their life as theirs.

The Adaptive Child usually internalizes that they are not inherently worthy. For many of my high achieving clients I work with, their Adaptive Child feels pressured to be perfect in order to be good enough or loved. Often their tendency to people please teaches them to become invisible and hide who they really are in order to avoid rejection, disappointment, or abandonment.

The Adaptive Child is often very porous because they look to the other for approval and self-worth. Due to not having any power over their environment, they will often personalize how they were treated. For example, if they were abused emotionally or physically, they might perceive that they were defective in some way and deserved that treatment due to their misbehavior. If they were emotionally or physically neglected, then they might internalize that they are defective or not special enough to be seen.

The Adaptive Tween often feels defective or ugly by societal standards and might mask or hide who they are in order to be accepted. Other times, if they feel defective as a young child, the Adaptive Tween can sometimes intentionally harm others to hide their unlovability by bullying or rejecting others before they themselves can be rejected.

The *medium circle* represents the Functional Adult, symbolizing the wise adult who will have your back no matter what because they hold you in unconditional love while also holding you accountable for any harm you might inflict on another, regardless of intention. Nothing you can do or say will make you more or less loveable or valuable to your Functional Adult. As you are, you are enough. Your Functional Adult does not try to figure out who is right or wrong, who is better or worse. Perfection is not the Functional Adult's goal. The ideal is to be authentic in all relationships by embodying their sense of Self, while also valuing the other person as equal to them. Functional Adults understand that everyone makes mistakes, hold you accountable compassionately for any harm, know you have a right to have your needs met, understand how to advocate for your wants using non-violent communication, protect themselves from others, and protect others from themselves.

The *large circle* represents the Adaptive Teen, who often unconsciously internalizes societal expectations by internalizing how they were parented. Adaptive Teens, believing that they know best and hate being wrong, see the world in black and white, right and wrong, good and bad.

Internally, just like relationally, people can bounce back and forth between the small circle and the large circle—from insecure to grandiose. When you notice that any of your Adaptive Children might be driving the bus, the ultimate goal and regular practice is to mindfully move your Self back into the right-sized medium circle that is the "same as"—equal to— everyone else.

Many people I work with are successful people pleasing women, like Cathy, Maria, and myself, who learned to submit and disappoint themselves in order to gain the approval of those in authority – this is how they learned to get approval and love from their caregiver(s) when they were young.

For Cathy, one of the reasons why she came to me was to understand why she was so angry at her son. After her Boundary Healing process, she understood that her Wounded Baby and Adaptive Child never felt as important or loved as her older brother. Cathy learned that standing up for herself was pointless because her parents always sided with her brother. Even though Cathy performed better academically, her brother was praised for doing very little in comparison to what was expected from Cathy from a young age. In our work together, Cathy needed to right-size her Self-esteem by learning to take up more space by setting clear boundaries and expectations for both her children and her husband.

When Cathy's son Daniel expressed disappointment, Cathy practiced imagining holding her Adaptive Child in her arms. She would reparent her Adaptive Child by affirming that her value is not contingent on raising a compliant or happy child. Her value is inherent. Being a good parent does not mean she needs to please her child or to demonstrate that she is capable. Her job is to provide enough structure and support even if Daniel expresses anger or defiance. Her Adaptive Child needs to only look internally to Cathy's Functional Adult for unconditional love, not outwardly to her son, her husband, or to any external standard of parenting.

Cathy then regulated herself from her Adaptive Teen who would often rage at Daniel because she couldn't hold her boundaries. Cathy's rage was a result of perceiving herself as the victim of her child's moods. By centering her child's comfort, Cathy was often too porous by feeling responsible for her son's behaviors as representative of her value or success as a parent.

POROUS, RIGID, AND HEALTHY BOUNDARIES

Porous boundaries look like the two circles overlapping completely. They are absolutely appropriate for caregivers with young children, but never between adults. Due to the limited brain development and inability to understand the different factors of the environment, children need caregivers to feel into and attune to them to help them identify what they may need: food, bathroom, safety, rest, soothing, or connection. Mind reading and people pleasing are other examples of porous boundaries.

Children with emotionally absent, emotionally abusive, and/or physically abusive parents often have a skewed sense of boundaries. For example, my mother was too porous with me by crossing into my boundary and telling me my intentions without gaining clarification directly from me. As she constantly monitored how I performed tasks in all aspects of my life, I learned that it was okay to be porous with others by assessing and monitoring what other people did. Let me tell you that my roommate in college did not appreciate my taking on the responsibility of waking her up to get to her classes on time. I had learned to have the audacity that I knew better than my roommate did about her own life choices.

Porous boundaries, like mind reading or gaslighting, is never okay in adult relationships, especially with our partners or our own parents. Mind reading is a belief we have in young childhood that we know what another person is thinking or feeling. You might believe you are able to sense how someone is feeling, but that means you've crossed into someone else's boundary, which is not healthy. Instead, clarify with them by asking them directly. This reduces your emotional labor and potential for miscommunication.

If you notice that you are being porous with another person who is not your young child, then imagine getting back in your lane by moving the circles further apart, like a Venn diagram, rather than completely overlapping.

Rigid boundaries look like two circles completely separate with a line between, where there is no consideration for the other person. This boundary is appropriate when the child is moving into teen and young adulthood because they need to differentiate from their parents in order to internalize who they are outside of their parents. This is often a difficult transition because it brings up a sense of betrayal or disloyalty to the family system, and that is okay. This differentiation is necessary.

Rigid Boundaries are also appropriate in abusive or neglectful relationships. It is not okay for anyone to emotionally or physically abuse you. If they do not stop, it is appropriate and necessary to become very *boundaried* in order to stay safe. However, it is not okay to be in a rigid boundary as a way to control someone else. For example, if you are trying to punish someone for declining a request, pulling away into a rigid boundary is another way to withdraw love, and that is abusive.

The Venn diagram where the two circles overlap a small section represents a *Healthy Boundary*, where I maintain my sense of self and wholeness and where you maintain your sense of self and wholeness outside of me. The overlapping space is where we interact, communicate using non-violent communication, and make behavioral requests.

I am in charge of maintaining my psychological boundary: how I feel, what I want and don't want, who I am and how I express it, likes and dislikes. The other person is in charge of their own psychological boundary: how they feel, what they want and don't want, who they are and how they want to express themselves, likes and dislikes. And just like I've brought myself to my right-size, in my mind, I maintain the other person's equalness to me even if they are more privileged or in a place of power.

The work an individual does to right-size who they are is revolutionary when you consider the origin of this country. The United States was literally founded on the stealing of land, massacring of indigenous people, and exploiting enslaved people stolen from Africa. This colonization deemed the Black, Indigenous, People of Color as "savages"– as lesser than those of the European White Body. Throw in capitalism and patriarchy, and we get what we have today: an institutionalized government-sanctioned way of oppressing the majority of people in the United States.

Part of what motivates me to teach this framework to others is my belief in the urgency of this work. If the majority of those in the 99 percent do not take steps to collective liberation, then the impact of the status quo will be increased (if that's even possible), leading to even more extreme economic disparity (if you can even imagine that) and the eventual destruction of our planet. None of this should be a surprise.

This is why I invite you, dear reader, to take steps to move the needle toward social justice and collective liberation.

9

START DECOLONIZING AND REPARENTING NOW!

THE RISK OF STATUS QUO

For those who are too overwhelmed to consider taking these steps to heal your boundary, I completely understand. The exhaustion of daily living is real. For those of us who didn't have parents who cherished and emotionally supported us, adulting can feel like we're perpetually running on empty because our tank was *never* filled. But that's not adulting from a Functional Adult place; that is our Adaptive Children pretending to be an adult in order to survive.

Trust that I know the risk and resistance to continue on the path I've laid out for you. Writing this book has been an internal battle for me. Showing up and sharing my experience publicly in this way feels scary and vulnerable to my Adaptive Child and Adaptive Tween. Perceived as the perpetual foreigner, my Asian-American body learned to shrink down, stay under the radar, and never question authority, so challenging the status quo feels like putting a target on my back, especially as I live into my full authenticity.

If my Adaptive Child had her way, I never would have considered writing this book because she successfully adapted to have no dreams or personal goals beyond taking care of everyone around her. My Adaptive Tween has stayed small and porous by predicting people's disappointment, criticism, and rejection. My Adaptive Teen has been in full writer's block due to her perfectionism and fear of appearing arrogant or disloyal to her mom. In order to survive, all of my Adaptive Children have learned to tolerate and expect low-grade misery, high levels of stress, and very little joy. When you're used to famine, crumbs seem like a feast.

The loneliness and isolation of the pandemic retriggered my childhood trauma and my Functional Adult stepped in to put an end to continuing the cycle of violence and neglect. As I healed my boundary, the life I created started falling apart. I was used to waking up hating my life, so when I started considering and prioritizing my needs and dreams, the uncharacteristic changes made sense.

My Functional Adult wanted more for me and wanted my daughters to see what was possible for their mom. So when I actively put my Functional Adult in the driver's seat, I slowly made decisions that moved me from the life I hated towards a life I loved.

Here are some of the things that I navigated within a short amount of time: I stopped centering my helpfulness and started centering my joy. I went low-contact with my family of origin. I ended my marriage and worked towards a healthier and happier co-parenting partnership. I changed the way that I work as a Mental Health Counselor to avoid codependency and burning out. I hired staff to do the tasks I hated. I invested in business classes so that I could work smarter and allow my money to work for me. I came out to my children and coparent as Queer. I ended friendships with people who weren't willing to be anti-racist. And last but not least, I got a puppy!

My Adaptive Children would have been fine with the status quo because survival was always their goal, but my Functional Adult refused to tolerate low-grade misery any longer. Rather than just survive, my Functional Adult wanted more!

Toni Jones, a brilliant singer and songwriter, has a song I try to live by: "Healing is not my life's purpose." For so long, my work as a therapist was to help people heal, but healing is centering the trauma and trying to adapt around it. My life's purpose is to help people reconnect to and celebrate who they really are and unlearn how we were taught to behave. My hope now is to embody a new worldview that is grounded in equality, non-violence, freedom, social responsibility, and interdependence.

Remember, perfection is not the goal. Living—in full authenticity—is the goal. My life's purpose is not to heal my ancestors' trauma. My life's purpose is to live the life they wanted to live themselves and to embody freedom, joy, and choice for a better future. May their sacrifices not be in vain.

If you'd like to begin the process of boundary healing by re-membering your sense of Self, here are the steps:

START HERE: RIGHTS OF A CHILD

Read this to yourself in the mirror every morning when you wake and every evening when you go to sleep. This practice will start the process of connecting you to the rights that you, and everyone else on this planet, are born with.

1. I am precious. No more and no less than anyone else. As I am, I am enough.
2. I am imperfect. Humans are meant to be perfectly imperfect.

3. I am vulnerable. I deserve to protect myself from abuse and neglect. Others deserve to be protected from abuse and neglect as well.

4. I commit to being interdependent. As social creatures, we are meant to live in community. We are connected to and responsible for each other and our planet.

5. I am allowed to be spontaneous and open. Others are also allowed that same freedom. Living in my full authenticity is a gift to the world.

STEP 1: IDENTIFY WHO'S DRIVING THE BUS

If you are exhausted, stressed, zoned out, desperate, rageful, overwhelmed, which are signs of dysregulation, then you likely have one of your Adaptive Children driving the bus influencing how you perceive the situation and limiting the possible solutions. The Wounded Baby and Adaptive Child will always internalize that there is something defective or wrong with them and feel like they can contort themselves in order to stay safe. The Adaptive Tween needs to feel socially accepted for who they are, since their task is to figure that out. The Adaptive Teen needs to learn to trust themselves and be able to hold themselves and others accountable for harm without throwing anyone under the bus. Since the Adaptive Children are a function of survival, this is another way of acknowledging that you are likely in your limbic system, the fight/flight/freeze/fawn part of your brain that won't have access to the full resources and perspective of your prefrontal cortex, or your wise mind, where the Functional Adult has access to creative solutions and moderate ways of responding.

STEP 2: PUT YOUR FUNCTIONAL ADULT BEHIND THE WHEEL

The practice of calming your brain and body will move you towards cultivating your Functional Adult, who is the best at relating to others in a non-violent way. Remember, if your Adaptive Children try to get their needs met from someone, it likely won't be in the right way because they actually needed it from their parents. The only person who can provide them what they need in the way they need now is your Functional Adult.

This isn't to say that you can't ask for what you need. In interdependence, we need to be able to provide mutual aid and community care. From the place of Functional Adult, you're able to connect with others in a way that is not oppressive or submissive, but from a place of equality.

First, regulate yourself to your Functional Adult by scanning your body for sensations and then exhaling on a count of six with a natural inhale for a few breaths while looking around the room. Orienting yourself to the space that you are in will help you get back in your body and remind yourself that you are not in imminent danger. This is the Functional Adult that you will be cultivating.

From this place of calm, imagine that you have your Wounded Baby swaddled in one hand, your Adaptive Child sitting in your lap, and your Adaptive Tween sitting across from you, facing you. Your Adaptive Teen is sitting next to you, not able to make eye contact.

There's no set order to connect with these Inner Children, so you can sense and see who would like your attention first. For me, I often need to connect with my Adaptive Teen first since they often try to control the desires and behaviors of the Adaptive Children and retraumatize them.

The Adaptive Teen needs respect, validation, and then a boundary. Try talking to this part like this: "I know how much you've needed to adapt to get us to this place in our lives. Thank you. I am so proud of how hard you've worked for so long. It makes sense that you're feeling so scared right now. You learned to be a chameleon and not have any needs. Showing up in this way feels really scary, like you're going to risk getting hurt. But right now you're already hurting. I, your Functional Adult, am here now and I'm taking the wheel. Thank you for driving us for so long. It's time for you to rest and learn to trust that we don't have to do this perfectly. It's also time for you to stop parenting the other Adaptive Children too. I know you're trying to keep them safe, but it's harmful to them. I've got them. Remember, I will have your back no matter what."

Your Adaptive Child needs physical affection and unconditional love, no matter what. For this part, try something like: "Sweetheart, I'm here now. Only look to me for your love and value. Not to your partner, not to the kids, not to your job, not to your friends. As you are, you are enough and I will always have your back. I'm the one you've been waiting for to love you. Nothing you can do or say will make me love you more. Nothing you can do or say will make me love you less, because I love you to the maximum."

Your Adaptive Tween needs to know that who they are will be welcomed and safe. Consider: "Hey! I see you! I love what I see on the outside and I love who you are on the inside. As you are, you are enough. No better and no worse than anyone else. Only look to me for your sense of belonging. I will vet everyone who gets close to us to make sure they are safe and will treat you with care and respect. Let me take the wheel so you can express yourself in the way that feels good to you and you can start meeting people who appreciate you fully."

Your Wounded Baby needs to be wanted and cared for by someone loving and safe. Communicate: "I am so excited you are here! You are my perfect baby. No matter how much you cry, no matter the mess, I will love you and cherish you and protect you. I happily build a beautiful life for you."

STEP 3: RIGHT-SIZE YOUR SELF BACK INTO A HEALTHY BOUNDARY

Figure out if you are in your right-sized boundary with whomever you are dealing with. Make sure you visualize right sizing you and the people you are dealing with. Then, make sure that the other person's response informs your next boundary: do you become more porous and allow them to be closer, or do you make your boundary more rigid and distance yourself?

Remember that healthy boundaries are when you experience your Self as equal to and as precious as another. You and everyone else is inherently worthy and special—no more and no less. Everyone has a right to express themselves and pursue their life as long as it does not negatively impact the rights of another human being. It is okay to make others uncomfortable. Adults have the capacity to deal with discomfort, especially if it's in relationship to one of your needs. Safety always trumps comfort.

Healthy boundaries are also about sharing your experience in appropriate ways that do not over-burden or disregard the other person. If your dynamic is too porous, here is what you need to do: After you right-size yourself bigger or smaller, then pull yourself away from the other person to differentiate rather than stay enmeshed. If the dynamic is too rigid, where the other person's feelings or needs are disre-garded, then the task is to become a bit more porous to build empathy for the other person. However, if there is abuse or neglect in the dynamic, then having a rigid boundary is appropriate.

Aim for the Venn diagram where both of you are of equal size and importance. Each of you is respon-sible for your feelings and regulating yourself so that you don't withdraw from or rage at someone you care about. You are also responsible for setting your own boundaries and advocating for your needs and wants in a respectful way. The shared space between is the collaboration and respectful communication as you negotiate shared goals and desires.

STEP 4: USE NON-VIOLENT COMMUNICATION TO CONNECT TO OTHERS

Share to be known, not to be right. Non-violent communication has changed my life because I have the skills to connect with anyone. We were recently picked up in an Uber by this older white man in an old school Buick with military bullets hanging from the rearview mirror. He was silent when we entered the car. No small talk. No eye contact. Nothing. With the increase in Asian hate crimes, my daughters were terrified and were texting me so we wouldn't be over-heard: "I'm scared."

I took a deep breath and said, "Sir. When I see these enormous bullets hanging from your rearview mirror, the story I make up is that you might want to tell us why. Can you tell us the story of those bullets?" That invitation to connect authentically brightened his eyes. After he told me about the war in the former Soviet Union, the long lines for rations, and his immigration to Boston, he told me that the bullets remind him that things can change at any moment. "When things change," he said, "stay open to what comes next. Stay creative."

In a brief twenty-minute car ride, I was able to meet a fellow comrade who had a beautiful message for me. My kids were relieved and so enamored by this kind man in the very sketchy Buick.

Non-violent communication can stop the cycle of violence.

Every day, we can write people off with our quick internalized biases, or we can show up in our fullness, inviting others that they are safe to do the same.

Writing this book has been a battle for me. Showing up fully and sharing my experience feels terrifying and vulnerable to my Adaptive Child and Adaptive Tween. They've learned to shrink down and stay under the radar. My Adaptive Teen has been rewriting the first three chapters over and over again to make sure I phrase it in a way that can help as many people as possible. See, my Adaptive Children have all learned to be invisible and helpful—to tolerate low-grade misery, high levels of stress, and very little rest and recovery.

What I know now is that there is no "one right way" to live one's life. If I decide to live from my Adaptive Children, I already know the outcome. I will wake up hating my life. It's been familiar since childhood. It's the unconscious epigenetic legacy I inherited. Like Cathy and Maria, we've all inherited this way of being in the world. Some have access to a bit more luxury and intergenerational wealth than others, but at the core, especially for the marginalized, we have been running on empty for generations.

Often, clients will look to me as if I have the answer guide for them. I am not omniscient. I am not perfect. I am struggling and unsure just like everyone else out there. Here's the reminder I give them: There is no answer guide that gets pulled out and referenced at your funeral. You are in the driver's seat of your own life. (If you don't think you are, then one of your Adaptive Children is at the Wheel.) Your body is the map. You are free to revisit familiar territory and fight over scraps, and you are free to forge new paths towards building authentic connections, experience true joy, and cultivate abundance by seeing yourself as an equal part of the larger whole. Your particular light is needed, especially right now.

Regardless of what you decide, remember that you are not alone and there is nothing wrong with you. As you are, you are enough.

AUTHOR'S NOTE

When I wrote the original book in 2023, I thought things were quite dire. I mentioned that boundary healing was urgent and required a grounded "functional adult" response so that we can break unconscious cycles of oppression and domination. Now, as I narrate this audiobook, the world feels even more bleak.

Thankfully, through my own work managing complex post-traumatic stress disorder, alongside my work with hundreds of clients paralyzed by decision fatigue and overwhelm, I know rock bottom is solid ground.

The release and discussion of the Epstein files have resurfaced a truth many already knew in their bones: "absolute power corrupts absolutely" (Lord Acton). Resource hoarding requires abuse of power.

Corruption requires complicity. Repeating history requires staying unconscious.

The spectacle of it is shocking, but the pattern is ancient.

Meanwhile, families across this country are still living with the terror of sudden ICE abductions—doors knocked down at dawn, children coming home to empty houses, entire communities bracing for disappearance as a daily possibility.

It would be easy to treat these as separate crises. A scandal among elites. A policy debate about immigration. But they are not separate. They are expressions of the same unresolved issues hidden away in our history, destined to repeat over and over again.

We are living inside the long arc of colonialism—a structure built on domination, extraction, and the normalization of violated boundaries. Land taken without consent. Bodies used without consent. Labor extracted without consent. Families separated without consent. Truth obscured without consent.

When we understand this historically, we stop being surprised. But we should never stop being disturbed and outraged.

Colonialism is not just an event in the past; it is a relational blueprint which teaches that power entitles you to take. That wealth exempts you from accountability. That some bodies are disposable. That silence is safer than truth. That survival requires silence.

These beliefs do not live only in institutions. They live in our nervous systems.

If you have ever struggled to say no, you are not alone.

If you have ever doubted your reality in the face of authority, you are not crazy.

If you have ever felt frozen while something wrong unfolded, you are not weak.

If you have ever tolerated harm because you feared the cost of resistance, you are not broken.

You are patterned.

The same dynamics that allow abuse to flourish at the highest levels are the ones that shape intimate relationships. The same fear that keeps communities silent is the fear that keeps individuals from enforcing their boundaries. The same dissociation that allows a nation to justify family separation is the dissociation that allows us to override our own limits.

This is why boundary healing is not self-help fluff. It is the real and worthwhile work of decolonizing.

When a child grows up in a family system shaped by trauma—whether that trauma comes from war, migration, racialized violence, poverty, or assimilation—they learn to survive by adapting. They learn when to shrink, when to appease, when to harden, and when to disconnect. These adaptations are intelligent. They are protective. And they are often inherited.

Unhealed trauma seeks familiarity. It recreates power imbalances. It normalizes boundary violations. It confuses intensity with intimacy by calling coercion "love" and control "safety." On a collective level, it elects leaders who mirror these dynamics. It perpetuates systems that enact them.

The Epstein scandal exposes how long abuse can be hidden when wealth and influence form a shield. ICE abductions expose how easily entire communities can be rendered vulnerable when their humanity is politicized. Both reveal the fragility of our ethical spine as a culture.

And both confront us with a question: Where are our boundaries?

Not just legally; not just politically. But emotionally, psychologically, and spiritually.

Do we know when something violates our values?

Do we trust ourselves enough to act?

Can we tolerate the discomfort of dissent?

Can we metabolize rage without turning it into cruelty?

Can we grieve without collapsing into despair?

Boundary work is the practice of rebuilding our ethical spine from the inside out.

It is learning to sense the moment when something is not right—and staying present.

It is differentiating between fear that protects and fear that imprisons.

It is interrupting inherited patterns of silence, compliance, or domination.

It is repairing after harm instead of denying it.

It is refusing to confuse power with worth.

When enough individuals strengthen their internal boundaries, collective boundaries become possible. Institutions only change when the people within them change. Culture only shifts when our nervous systems can tolerate a new way of relating.

This is not about becoming harder. It is about becoming clearer.

Clear about consent.

Clear about accountability.

Clear about whose comfort has historically been prioritized.

Clear about the cost of pretending not to see.

The urgency of this moment is not just political—it is psychological. Trauma that is not processed becomes policy. Dissociation that is not healed becomes ideology. Unexamined power becomes entitlement.

We cannot build a just society with colonized nervous systems.

Healing is not withdrawal from the world. It is preparation to engage it without reenacting the very harm we oppose. When we tend to our individual boundaries, we disrupt ancestral scripts. When we metabolize inherited trauma, we reduce the likelihood that we will pass it forward. When we learn to repair after rupture, we create relational models that do not depend on domination.

The work is intimate. And it is collective.

We do not break cycles of harm by shaming ourselves or each other. We break them by increasing our capacity—to feel, to name, to confront, to hold complexity, to stay in relationship without abandoning our integrity.

The systems we are outraged by are not sustained by monsters alone. They are sustained by unhealed patterns, by fear of exclusion, by learned helplessness, and by the normalization of violated boundaries.

Which means they can be undone.

Not overnight. Not without resistance. But undone nonetheless.

This book is an invitation to begin—or to deepen—that undoing.

To decolonize your relationships.

To reclaim your internal authority.

To strengthen your emotional and psychological boundaries.

To grieve what has been normalized.

To refuse what has been inherited.

To embody a different way of relating—one that

does not require someone else's erasure to secure your safety.

We cannot control the headlines, but we can interrupt the patterns that make those headlines possible. The cycle ends here.

That is where the revolution begins: inside you, alongside me, reconnecting us.

WORKS CITED/FURTHER READING

Gifts From a Challenging Childhood: Creating A Practice for Becoming Your Healthiest Self, Jan Bergstrom, LMHC

My Grandmother's Hands: Racialized Trauma and the Pathway to Mending Our Hearts and Bodies, Resmaa Menakem

Nonviolent Communication: Create Your Life, Your Relationships, and Your World in Harmony with Your Values, Marshall B. Rosenberg, PhD

"I See Me Mantras" Album by Toni Jones

ACKNOWLEDGMENTS

At the center of the Chinese character of love 愛 is the character for heart 心. My life's purpose is about joyfully restoring our connection to our hearts, our humanity, and with each other. I could not have survived this long, discovered my meaningful contribution to my community, or written this book without the loving hearts of so many.

To all my Black elders and siblings who prepared the road for so many of us, thank you for your joy, your sacrifice, your labor, your wisdom, and especially your love. To Ronda and Sonya, your calling me in to be accountable for my internalized racism shook me to the core—waking me from my ignorant slumber and inviting me to do better. Challenge accepted.

To all my communities of mothers in Massachusetts: Momoirs, Thompson Tuesdays, Raising Children of Color, PTO, and Mutual Aid. Together, we can do anything. Particular thanks to Kate, Jacquie, Linda, Christy, Laura, Louise, and Anne and so many more.

To my FCS faith community, especially Jenn and

Michael. Thank you for connecting me to the version of God whose love is unconditional and demands for us all to do better – to protect and empower the most vulnerable among us.

To my friends near and far who texted, dropped off food, and spoon fed me words of encouragement. You kept my cup filled enough to keep going. Kate and Rafael, thank you for opening your home and hearth to me so often when I needed a quiet place to dream about my future Self.

To Janus, my white male therapist who helps me feel safe in my body. Will wonders never cease! Rest and belly laughter is my new therapy, thanks to you.

To those who made this book possible: Angela, Natasa, and Shauna. Wow, thank goodness for your skillset!

To Melissa and Ian, your steady companionship, dry humor, and unconditional love, especially when I was the most alone, transformed me. You model a love that I am now capable of receiving and giving.

To Ramon, my co-parent, we found each other at just the right time. I will be forever grateful to you and for the time we had together in marriage. Through our love, we brought two incredible children, our teachers, into the world. What gifts! May the next part of our journey together deepen our friendship and continue to guide us to be the parents our kids deserve.

To Sofia with an F. Your full name means wisdom and peace. Wise beyond your years and with such a pure heart. My own heart swells with so much pride to witness you stand up for yourself and others because you know that peace does not mean staying silent in the face of injustice.

To Kaia, a natural born leader and knows how to include everyone effortlessly and authentically. You, who can get anyone to do anything exactly at the time you want, have been my greatest teacher. Thank you for showing me the gift of embodied joy and creativity to solve any problem.

To Luna, our newish puppy. You are my reminder that there is so much more to life than work. Your companionship, especially in the middle of this book writing process, renews my faith in the Universe that everything is unfolding as it is meant to.

To my Aunt Sherri, who introduced me to Family Constellations, and helped me to uncover so many truths about myself, I am so grateful for your guidance.

To my Family in Colorado and Taiwan, we may be separated for so many different reasons, but always know that I hold you close in my heart, wish you all the best, and appreciate all that you have done to make me and my life what is it today.

To my mother who gave me life and made my calling possible. As I mature and understand the impact of collective trauma, I hold so much respect, appreciation, and love for you. Mama, 媽媽, 謝謝妳. Your sacrifice will not be wasted or repeated. I will always be your loving daughter, and you my 媽媽.

And to my father, who loved me with his quiet smile and with his food. Daddy, whatever I wanted to eat, you made meals for me without any resentment or guilt. I carry you and your generosity in my heart always and in the bellies of your grandchildren. Your suffering was not in vain. I turned that bitterness you taught me to swallow into a feast for so many.

我愛你

Judy Hu, LMHC is a Licensed Mental Health Counselor turned Boundary Coach based in Massachusetts with over two decades of clinical experience.

Judy's life was shaped by trying to fit into boxes laid out in front of her by her immigrant family, by her "normal" peers, and by a society based on oppression. None of those boxes or expectations fit. Trying to mask feelings of being an impostor and not good enough, she landed at an all-time low and finally chose her Self. Her detoxification from co-dependence allowed a clear view of the systems that imprisoned her. A wounded healer at heart, she created a step-by-step framework to guide others to their own joyful liberation.

She completed her masters at Lesley University in Expressive Arts. Continuing education, trainings, and her endless curiosity allow her to stay up-to-date on current research and cutting-edge practices.

Serving people all over the world, Judy utilizes traditional talk therapy, mindfulness, hypnosis, somatic practices, family constellations, developmental and relational trauma therapy, EMDR, and other trauma-informed interventions.

An avid lover of board games and the show *Bluey*, Judy is a mother of two fiercely free teens and a lively dog, Luna. Proudly, Judy is a cycle breaker and disruptor.

Website: http://theboundaryrevolution.com

Email: Judy@JudyHuBoundaryCoach.com

FB: https://www.facebook.com/JudyHuCounseling

IG: https://www.instagram.com/judyhuboundarycoach/

TikTok: https://www.tiktok.com/@judyhuboundarycoach

LinkedIn: https://www.linkedin.com/in/judyhuboundarycoach/

Thank you for listening to *The Boundary Revolution: Decolonize Your Relationships and Discover a New Path to Joy*. It is an honor to share my story, my clients anonymized stories, stories my thoughts with you in this book. I hope my Psychological Boundaries Framework provides clear steps for you to decolonize and detoxify from within so that you may find a new path to joy and liberation. My wish is that collectively we remember to care for ourselves, each other, and our planet. It is never too late and the urgency is real.

As a gift to you, please visit https://thebound aryrevolution.com/gift-to-reader to download my PDF guide to help you with boundaries and general tips on how to reparent your internal adaptive children, so you can mature your functional adult and transform your life. This cheat sheet is great to put on your fridge or phone so the steps are right there.

If you'd like more support, consider joining my signature Cycle Breaker group coaching program, where you commit to four months of weekly practice within a brave space of like-minded people who are birthing a new way of being in the world, one that centers equality, nonviolence, social responsibility, and interdependence. You're invited to one complementary session to try it out. I also provide private boundary healing intensives and one-on-one sessions where we center your joyful living.

Email me at Judy@JudyHuBoundaryCoach.com. Until then, remember, as you are, you are enough.

In love and solidarity,

Judy